ENTREPRENEURSHIP
An Introduction

John Monyjok Maluth

Copyright © 2024 John Monyjok Maluth

*

ISBN: 9798323649549

Discipleship Press

Web: www.discipleshippress.wordpress.com
Email: maluthabiel@gmail.com

~~*~~

+254 797 624 994
+211 927 145 394

P.O. Box 28448-00100, Nairobi Kenya

All rights reserved. No part of this book may be reproduced, stored in a retrieval system, or transmitted in any or by any means – electronic, mechanical, photocopying, recording, or otherwise- without prior permission in writing from the copyright holder.

DISCLAIMER:

This is a work of fiction. While inspired by real-world events, places, or concepts, the story and characters are entirely fictional. Any resemblance to actual persons, living or dead, or actual events is unintentional.

DISCLAIMER

This book teaches entrepreneurship through an example-driven story. The characters, scenes, and conversations are created to make business lessons practical and memorable. Any resemblance to real persons or events is coincidental.

DEDICATION

I dedicate this book to the builder who starts small, keeps learning, and refuses to quit. To the tailor, the trader, the designer, the service provider, the creator, the shop owner, the freelancer, and the online seller. If your hands are tired but your dream is still alive, this book is for you.

AUTHOR'S NOTE

I am Panyim (John), and I will teach you entrepreneurship the way I learned it: by doing, correcting, and doing again.

In these pages, I use a simple teaching story to carry real business principles. Nyakor and the other names you will meet are examples. Their role is to show decisions, mistakes, and better moves, the same way a sample garment shows a pattern before we cut the expensive fabric.

If you only read, you will feel motivated for a day. If you read and apply, you will build something that can feed you for years.

HOW TO USE THIS BOOK

Read with a notebook beside you.
After every chapter, write down:
What I will implement this week.
What I will stop doing this week.
What I will measure so I do not guess.

Keep it simple. Entrepreneurship is not magic. It is a set of repeatable actions:
Make an offer people want.
Put it in front of the right people.
Earn trust.
Deliver well.
Improve based on results.

CONTENTS

PART ONE: THE DIGITAL MARKETPLACE 1

  CHAPTER ONE: THE POWER OF DIGITAL MARKETING 1
  CHAPTER TWO: UNDERSTANDING TARGET AUDIENCE 11
  WHY MOST SMALL BUSINESSES STAY STUCK 11
  WHAT I TEACH: HOW I FIND THE IDEAL CUSTOMER (SIMPLE MARKET RESEARCH + PLATFORM DATA) 12
  WHAT YOU BUILD: THE IDEAL CUSTOMER PAGE 15
  WHAT YOU ALSO BUILD: KEYWORDS AND CONVERSATION TOPICS 18
  PRACTICE: STOP CHASING EVERYONE, CHOOSE THE RIGHT PEOPLE, SPEAK DIRECTLY 20
  A SHORT EXAMPLE YOU CAN LEARN FROM 22
  CHAPTER TWO SUMMARY (WHAT YOU SHOULD HAVE NOW) 23
  CHAPTER THREE: NAVIGATING THE DIGITAL ECOSYSTEM 24
  WHAT I TEACH: HOW I CHOOSE PLATFORMS AND CONNECT THEM INTO ONE WORKING SYSTEM 24
  YOUR DIGITAL HOME VS RENTED SPACE 26
  WHAT YOU BUILD: YOUR DIGITAL HOME MAP 27
  CONNECTING THE SYSTEM: WEBSITE, SOCIAL, EMAIL, PAYMENTS, DELIVERY 29
  VISIBILITY: SEO AND CONSISTENT ENGAGEMENT 32
  PRACTICE: CHOOSE PLATFORMS, SET UP THE BASICS, AND KEEP IT CONSISTENT 33
  THE POINT OF THE DIGITAL ECOSYSTEM 36

PART TWO: BUILDING YOUR ONLINE PRESENCE 36

  FIELD GUIDE (BRAND ASSETS) 36
  A USER'S GUIDE TO PHOTOGRAPHY FOR YOUR ONLINE BUSINESS 36
  1) THE PURPOSE OF BUSINESS PHOTOGRAPHY 37
  2) LIGHT: THE CHEAPEST UPGRADE YOU CAN MAKE 37
  USE NATURAL LIGHT FIRST 38
  BEST TIMES FOR OUTDOOR PHOTOS 38
  THE SIMPLE TEST FOR GOOD LIGHT 38
  3) BACKGROUND: REMOVE CLUTTER, INCREASE TRUST 38
  CHOOSE A SIMPLE BACKGROUND 39
  4) FRAMING: HOW TO POSITION THE PRODUCT SO IT SELLS 39
  USE THESE FOUR SHOT TYPES (ROTATE THEM) 39
  KEEP YOUR HORIZON STRAIGHT 40
  LEAVE BREATHING SPACE 41
  5) CONSISTENCY: THE HIDDEN POWER OF A STRONG FEED 41
  HOW I KEEP MY FEED CONSISTENT 41
  6) EDITING: IMPROVE WITHOUT LYING 42
  BASIC EDITS THAT HELP 42
  7) PHONE CAMERA SETTINGS THAT ACTUALLY MATTER 42
  CLEAN YOUR LENS 42

- USE THE BACK CAMERA 42
- TAP TO FOCUS 42
- AVOID DIGITAL ZOOM 42
- USE PORTRAIT MODE CAREFULLY 43
- 8) WHAT TO PHOTOGRAPH (SO YOU NEVER RUN OUT OF CONTENT) 43
- 9) CAPTIONS THAT SELL WITHOUT SOUNDING DESPERATE 44
- MY CAPTION STRUCTURE (SIMPLE AND REPEATABLE) 44
- 10) PRICING AND PHOTOGRAPHY: SHOW VALUE, NOT CHEAPNESS 45
- 11) PROOF PHOTOS: HOW TO USE CUSTOMERS ETHICALLY AND EFFECTIVELY .. 45
- 12) A SIMPLE WEEKLY PHOTOGRAPHY PLAN 46
- 13) QUICK PHOTOGRAPHY CHECKLIST (USE BEFORE POSTING) 46
- 14) THE DEEPER LESSON BEHIND PHOTOGRAPHY 47

PART TWO: BUILDING YOUR ONLINE PRESENCE 48

- CHAPTER FIVE: CREATING ENGAGING CONTENT 48
- 1) THE REAL PURPOSE OF CONTENT FOR BUSINESS 48
- 2) THE SHIFT: FROM POSTING PRODUCTS TO PUBLISHING A TRUST-BUILDING FEED 49
- 3) WHAT YOU BUILD: A CONTENT RHYTHM YOU CAN KEEP 50
- STEP 1: CHOOSE WEEKLY THEMES (SIMPLE, NOT COMPLICATED) 50
- STEP 2: CHOOSE REUSABLE POST TYPES (THIS STOPS CONTENT STRESS) 51
- STEP 3: BUILD A SIMPLE CALENDAR (THE SMALLEST SYSTEM THAT WORKS) .. 52
- 4) WHAT YOU BUILD: A SYSTEM FOR CUSTOMER PHOTOS AND TESTIMONIALS 53
- STEP 1: ASK AT THE RIGHT TIME 53
- STEP 2: MAKE IT EASY FOR THE CUSTOMER 53
- STEP 3: ORGANIZE YOUR PROOF ASSETS 54
- STEP 4: USE PROOF ETHICALLY 54
- 5) THE THREE CONTENT ENGINES THAT BUILD TRUST 54
- A) BEHIND-THE-SCENES CONTENT (PROCESS BUILDS CREDIBILITY) 55
- B) CUSTOMER STORY CONTENT (RESULTS BUILD PROOF) 55
- C) EDUCATIONAL CONTENT (TEACHING BUILDS AUTHORITY) 56
- 6) THE CONTENT TONE: ENGAGING WITHOUT SOUNDING DESPERATE 56
- 7) WHAT ENGAGING CONTENT LOOKS LIKE IN PRACTICE 57
- 8) PRACTICE: YOUR WEEKLY CONTENT DISCIPLINE 58
- YOUR WEEKLY CHECKLIST (COPY) 58
- 9) HOW TO AVOID BURNOUT WHILE POSTING CONSISTENTLY 59
- CHAPTER FIVE SUMMARY (WHAT YOU SHOULD HAVE NOW) 60

PART TWO: BUILDING YOUR ONLINE PRESENCE 61

- CHAPTER SIX: THE ART OF STORYTELLING 61
- 1) WHY STORYTELLING MAKES CUSTOMERS PAY MORE AND COMPLAIN LESS .. 62
- 2) STORYTELLING IS NOT LONG WRITING. IT IS CLEAR MEANING 62
- 3) WHAT YOU BUILD: THE STORYTELLING TOOLKIT 63
- A) ORIGIN STORY (WHY I STARTED AND WHAT I STAND FOR) 63
- B) PRODUCT STORY (WHY THIS PRODUCT EXISTS AND WHAT IT SAYS) 64

C) Customer transformation story (the real proof narrative) 65
4) The story bank: your endless content library 66
What goes into the story bank 67
How I capture stories (simple method) 67
5) Turning story into content: simple formats 68
6) The discipline: meaning without manipulation 68
7) Practice: write one short brand story and pair it with one product post ..68
Step 1: Write your short brand story (use this template).............................69
Step 2: Pair it with a product post (use this structure) 69
8) Quick checklist for story-based content 70
Chapter Six summary (what you should have now)...70

PART THREE: ENGAGING YOUR AUDIENCE 71

Chapter Seven: Social Media Mastery 71
1) What "social media mastery" really means..72
2) The mindset shift: I am not competing for attention, I am building trust ..72
3) The three pillars of social media mastery...73
4) What I teach: using social platforms to build community, not noise 73
A) Engagement habits (the daily actions that build trust) 73
B) Collaborations (borrow trust, multiply reach) 76
C) Customer-driven content (turn buyers into marketing) 77
5) What you build: a platform plan 78
Step 1: Choose your primary platform 78
Step 2: Define your content mix 79
Step 3: Choose a posting rhythm you can sustain...79
Step 4: Define the purpose of each post..79
6) What you build: a simple engagement schedule 80
Daily engagement schedule (30 to 45 minutes total).....................................80
Weekly engagement schedule (one deeper session).....................................81
7) Practice: reply fast, ask good questions, feature customers, invite them
into the journey..81
Practice 1: Reply fast with a professional structure 81
Practice 2: Ask questions that guide buying 82
Practice 3: Feature customers weekly 82
Practice 4: Invite customers into the journey...82
8) Common mistakes that turn social media into noise 82
9) How to measure progress (what matters, not vanity) 83
10) Final word: community is built by repeated respect................................83
Field Guides (Platform Playbooks)..85
User's Guide: How to Use Instagram to Build Your Brand 85
User's Guide: Building a WhatsApp Community for Your Business..........88
User's Guide: How to Use X to Boost Your Business 92
A User's Guide to LinkedIn for Business Growth...94
Closing note I use across all platforms...97

- CHAPTER EIGHT: THE POWER OF MOBILE MARKETING 98
- WHY MOBILE WINS IN REAL BUSINESS 98
- THE MOBILE-FIRST MINDSET: I BUILD A PATH, NOT A PILE OF TOOLS 99
- THE MOBILE TOOLS I RELY ON (AND WHY) 100
- WHATSAPP AS THE SALES ENGINE 100
- SET UP WHATSAPP BUSINESS THE RIGHT WAY 100
- USE THESE WHATSAPP BUSINESS TOOLS TO SAVE TIME AND INCREASE TRUST 101
- THE BIGGEST RULE: KEEP WHATSAPP LOW-FRICTION 102
- MOBILE-FRIENDLY PAGES THAT LOAD FAST AND SELL CLEARLY 103
- WHAT A MOBILE-FRIENDLY PAGE MUST INCLUDE 103
- HOW I KEEP MOBILE PAGES FAST, ESPECIALLY WITH WEAK INTERNET 103
- MOBILE PAYMENTS: REMOVE FRICTION, INCREASE CONFIDENCE 104
- PAYMENT OPTIONS THAT WORK WELL ON MOBILE 104
- THE MOST IMPORTANT PAYMENT PRACTICE: CONFIRM AND DOCUMENT 104
- MOBILE MARKETING IN UNSTABLE CONNECTIVITY: HOW I STAY RELIABLE WHEN THE NETWORK IS NOT 105
- REDUNDANCY MEANS I PLAN FOR FAILURE 105
- WHAT YOU BUILD: A MOBILE-FIRST COMMUNICATION FLOW 106
- STAGE 1: INQUIRY 106
- STAGE 2: QUALIFICATION 107
- STAGE 3: PRICING AND OPTIONS 107
- STAGE 4: ORDER CONFIRMATION 107
- STAGE 5: DELIVERY UPDATES 108
- STAGE 6: AFTERCARE AND RETENTION 109
- WHAT YOU BUILD: A SIMPLE CUSTOMER BROADCAST ROUTINE 109
- MY BROADCAST RULES 109
- THE WEEKLY BROADCAST STRUCTURE I RECOMMEND 109
- SEGMENTING YOUR BROADCAST (OPTIONAL, BUT POWERFUL) 110
- PRACTICE: SET UP WHATSAPP BUSINESS TOOLS, CREATE A QUICK PRODUCT CATALOG, BUILD A WEEKLY MESSAGE PLAN 110
- PRACTICE STEP 1: SET UP WHATSAPP BUSINESS TOOLS 110
- PRACTICE STEP 2: CREATE A QUICK PRODUCT CATALOG 111
- PRACTICE STEP 3: BUILD A WEEKLY MESSAGE PLAN 112
- THE MOBILE-FIRST ADVANTAGE: WHY THIS CHAPTER MATTERS 112
- CHAPTER NINE: BUILDING CUSTOMER RELATIONSHIPS 114
- 1) THE REAL MEANING OF CUSTOMER RELATIONSHIPS 114
- 2) THE RELATIONSHIP ECONOMY: WHY REPEAT CUSTOMERS MATTER 115
- 3) WHAT I TEACH: HOW I KEEP CUSTOMERS AFTER THE FIRST SALE 115
- A) SERVICE THAT FEELS PROFESSIONAL 116
- B) FOLLOW-UP THAT FEELS HUMAN 116
- C) COMMUNITY THAT FEELS SAFE 117
- D) FEEDBACK LOOPS THAT IMPROVE THE BUSINESS 117
- E) LOYALTY HABITS THAT REWARD REPEAT BEHAVIOR 118
- 4) WHAT YOU BUILD: A CUSTOMER JOURNEY PLAN 118

CUSTOMER JOURNEY PLAN (COPY AND FILL) 119
5) WHAT YOU BUILD: SIMPLE SCRIPTS FOR REPLIES, UPDATES, AND PROBLEM-SOLVING 120
A) BEFORE PURCHASE SCRIPTS 120
B) DURING PURCHASE SCRIPTS 121
C) AFTER PURCHASE SCRIPTS 121
D) PROBLEM-SOLVING SCRIPTS (THE RELATIONSHIP SAVER).........................122
6) PRACTICE: CREATE A FOLLOW-UP MESSAGE SEQUENCE 123
FOLLOW-UP SEQUENCE (COPY AND USE) 123
7) PRACTICE: INVITE REVIEWS THE RIGHT WAY 124
REVIEW REQUEST MESSAGE (COPY) 124
8) PRACTICE: TURN FEEDBACK INTO PRODUCT AND SERVICE IMPROVEMENTS 125
STEP 1: COLLECT FEEDBACK WEEKLY 125
STEP 2: IDENTIFY PATTERNS 125
STEP 3: CHOOSE ONE IMPROVEMENT PER WEEK 125
STEP 4: COMMUNICATE IMPROVEMENTS 126
9) LOYALTY HABITS THAT KEEP CUSTOMERS CLOSE 126
LOYALTY HABIT IDEAS (CHOOSE TWO) 126
10) THE RELATIONSHIP DASHBOARD: WHAT I TRACK.....................................127
11) THE FINAL LESSON: RELATIONSHIPS ARE A SYSTEM, NOT A MOOD 127

PART FOUR: MEASURING SUCCESS AND GROWTH 129

CHAPTER TEN: TRACKING YOUR RESULTS 129
1) WHY MOST ENTREPRENEURS STAY STUCK: THEY DO WORK, BUT THEY DON'T LEARN 129
2) THE TRUTH ABOUT "ANALYTICS": IT IS SIMPLY COUNTING WHAT MATTERS 130
3) THE FIVE STAGES I TRACK IN EVERY BUSINESS..131
4) WHAT YOU BUILD: THE ONE-PAGE SCORECARD 131
5) DEFINITIONS THAT KEEP YOUR TRACKING CLEAN 133
6) WHERE I GET THE NUMBERS (SIMPLE SOURCES) 134
7) THE KEY IDEA: LEADING METRICS VS LAGGING METRICS...........................135
8) LINKING RESULTS BACK TO ACTIONS (THE PART THAT MAKES TRACKING POWERFUL) 136
9) HOW I USE TRACKING TO DIAGNOSE BUSINESS PROBLEMS 137
10) WHAT YOU BUILD: THE WEEKLY REVIEW HABIT 138
11) THE SCORECARD IN ACTION: A SAMPLE WEEK 140
12) THE SIMPLEST WAY TO TRACK IN A NOTEBOOK (IF YOU HATE DIGITAL TOOLS) 142
13) PRACTICE: CHOOSE KEY METRICS, TRACK WEEKLY, LINK RESULTS BACK TO ACTIONS 143
14) THE FINAL LESSON: MEASUREMENT MAKES YOU PEACEFUL AND SHARP 144
CHAPTER ELEVEN: ADAPTING AND EVOLVING 145
1) THE MINDSET: STABILITY IS NOT REFUSING CHANGE, STABILITY IS MANAGING CHANGE
....146
2) WHY PANIC DESTROYS LEARNING 146
3) WHAT I TEACH: HOW I STAY RELEVANT WHEN THE WORLD SHIFTS 147
4) WHAT YOU BUILD: A LIGHTWEIGHT TESTING HABIT (ONE CHANGE AT A TIME) 151
5) WHAT YOU BUILD: A FEEDBACK SYSTEM (CUSTOMERS, PLATFORM DATA, SALES).....153
6) THE WEEKLY EXPERIMENT ENGINE: WHAT TO TEST (PRACTICAL LIST).....................155

7) How I avoid being late to trends without chasing trends 156
8) How I respond when a platform changes 156
9) How I handle new competitors without fear... 157
10) Practice: run one small experiment per week 158
11) Keep what works, drop what doesn't: the discipline of refinement........ 159
12) The final lesson: adapt with calm, evolve with evidence 159
Chapter Twelve: Beyond the Basics... 161
1) The difference between growth and expansion 161
2) The expansion mindset: stop thinking like a worker, start thinking like a builder 162
3) What I teach: how I go from online presence to real expansion 163
4) The expansion map: the four pillars I strengthen 165
5) What you build: a growth plan 167
The 90-Day Growth Plan (copy and fill)... 168
6) What you build: a delegation plan (tasks you should not keep doing alone) 169
7) Scaling systems: what must become "systemized" first 171
8) Entering new markets: the safest paths for expansion 173
9) Strengthening operations: how I protect quality while scaling............... 174
10) Building a brand community that can grow beyond me 175
11) Practice: choose one expansion path and build the system behind it........ 176
12) The final lesson: expansion is discipline, not excitement 177
IMPLEMENTATION SPRINTS (Work sections readers can follow) 179
The 7-Day Setup Sprint... 179
Day 1: Define your offer (what you sell, who it is for, why it matters) 180
Day 2: Define your audience (stop chasing everyone) 181
Day 3: Choose your main platform and set up your "home base" 181
Day 4: Build your first content pillars and post templates 182
Day 5: Publish your first two posts and practice engagement.................... 183
Day 6: Create your basic sales flow (inquiry to order)................................. 183
Day 7: Publish again, invite action, and set the weekly rhythm 184
The 30-Day Consistency Sprint 185
Week 1: Build your rhythm and protect your time...................................... 185
Week 2: Improve your message and your call to action 186
Week 3: Build your engagement system and your community habits 187
Week 4: Basic tracking and a simple weekly review 187
The 90-Day Growth Sprint.. 188
Month 1 (Days 1–30): Strengthen your foundation and start retention 188
Month 2 (Days 31–60): Add SEO and search visibility 189
Month 3 (Days 61–90): Partnerships, experiments, and expansion signals ..190
The sprint rule that keeps you from chasing shiny ideas 191
A closing instruction from me to you 191
FIELD GUIDE APPENDICES (Copy-ready tools) 192
Appendix A: Brand Identity Sheet Template (Copy-ready)........................192

Appendix B: Ideal Customer Sheet Template (Copy-ready) 194
Appendix C: Content Calendar Template (Copy-ready) 196
Appendix D: Photo and Caption Checklist (Copy-ready) 197
Appendix E: Instagram Checklist (Copy-ready) 198
Appendix F: WhatsApp Group Rules and Welcome Message Templates (Copy-ready) 199
Appendix G: Twitter (X) Posting Rhythm Template (Copy-ready) 200
Appendix H: LinkedIn Profile Checklist and Outreach Template (Copy-ready) 201
Appendix I: Customer Follow-up Scripts (Copy-ready) 202
Appendix J: Giveaway and User-Generated Content Plan Template (Copy-ready) 203
Appendix K: Weekly Scorecard Template and Review Questions (Copy-ready) 205

BACK MATTER 207

Final Note to the Reader 207
Leave a Review 208
Order and Bulk Copies (training and teams) 209
About the Author 210

PART ONE: THE DIGITAL MARKETPLACE
Chapter One: The Power of Digital Marketing

I want to start with a simple truth that most people miss.

A business used to grow mainly by geography. If you had a shop at the right corner, near the right road, close to the right market, people would pass by, notice you, and buy. Your "marketing" was the fact that you existed in a busy place. You were visible because of location.

Today, visibility is no longer guaranteed by location. Visibility is earned through attention.

That shift changes everything.

A tailor can sit in a small room with a single sewing machine and still sell to customers across a city, across a country, and sometimes across borders. A baker can sell out every weekend without a fancy storefront. A writer can sell books without a physical bookstore. A mechanic can become booked for weeks by showing his work online.

Not because they moved to a richer neighborhood, but because they learned how to capture attention and convert it into trust, then into sales.

That is what digital marketing does.

Digital marketing is not "being online." It is not "posting pictures." It is not "making noise."

Digital marketing is the skill of earning attention, earning trust, and guiding a person to a clear next step.

When you understand this, you stop feeling powerless. You stop blaming the economy every day. You stop waiting for luck.

Because attention can be built.

From "location only" to "location plus attention"
Let me paint the difference using an example.

Nyakor is a skilled tailor. She makes clean stitching. Her fits are sharp. Customers love her work. But she lives in a place where foot traffic is not heavy. She can sit the whole day and only three people pass by the door.

In the old model, she is stuck. Her skill is real, but her location limits her.

Now imagine the "location plus attention" model.

She still works in the same room. Same street. Same neighborhood. But now she posts short videos of her process: measuring, cutting, stitching, fitting. She shares before-and-after photos of clients who allowed it. She explains fabric choices in plain language. She posts customer feedback. She answers messages politely and fast.

Soon, people who have never stepped on her street begin to know her name. They start sending inquiries. Someone refers a friend. Another customer sees her work and asks for pricing. A bride-to-be wants fittings. A young professional wants two shirts every month.

Nyakor did not change location.

She added attention.

That is the new advantage of business in our time: you can build reach without owning expensive space.

Your location is still important, but it is no longer your ceiling.

Why attention matters more than you think
Attention is not a shallow thing. It is the gate to everything else.

If people do not notice you, they cannot consider you.
If they cannot consider you, they cannot trust you.
If they cannot trust you, they cannot buy.

Attention does not mean viral fame. It means consistent visibility among the right people.

Your goal is not to be known by everyone. Your goal is to be known by the people who need what you sell and can pay for it.

When you earn that kind of attention, your business starts to breathe. You get a pipeline of inquiries. You begin to choose customers instead of begging for customers. You gain the freedom to improve quality because sales are no longer random.

This is why digital marketing becomes a growth lever even for a small shop.

A "lever" is something small that moves something big. A short video can bring a customer. A clear product photo can bring an order. A simple story can build loyalty. A helpful tip can earn trust. One good message can start a relationship.

What digital marketing really is
Digital marketing is a set of actions that connect three things:

Your offer
Your audience
Your message

Then it uses a channel to deliver that message and a system to follow up.

That's it.

Many people complicate it and get lost. They chase every new platform. They buy tools they do not use. They copy big brands and feel discouraged.

I do the opposite.

I build from clarity.

What do I sell?
Who is it for?
Why does it matter?
Where do these people already spend time?
What message will make them stop and pay attention?
What is the next step I want them to take?

When you can answer those questions, you are not confused anymore. You are ready to build.

What you build in this chapter: a simple digital offer
Before we talk about a "plan," we must define what we are taking to the market.

A simple digital offer has three parts:

What you sell
Who it is for
Why it matters

That sounds too simple, but most businesses fail because this is unclear.

Let's tighten each part.

What you sell (say it in one sentence)
Do not say, "I sell many things."
Do not say, "I do everything."
Do not hide behind vague words like "solutions."

Say it plainly.

Examples:
I make custom office shirts for working men.
I bake celebration cakes for birthdays and weddings.
I design book covers for self-publishing authors.
I sell affordable skincare products for women with sensitive skin.
I offer phone repair and screen replacement within 24 hours.

Clear beats clever.

Who it is for (choose, do not guess)
Many people fear choosing because they think they will lose customers. But unclear targeting loses more customers than clear targeting ever will.

Pick a primary customer group.

Not "everyone."
Not "anyone with money."

Examples:
University students who want affordable fashion.
Office workers who need reliable weekly meal prep.
New parents who need baby photography.
Small business owners who want simple websites.
Church leaders who want printed programs and banners.

When you choose, your message becomes sharp.

Why it matters (the benefit and the feeling)
People do not buy a product only. They buy the outcome and the feeling.

A shirt is not just cloth. It is confidence.
A cake is not just sugar. It is celebration.
A website is not just design. It is credibility.
A repaired phone is not just a device. It is access to life.

Your "why it matters" is the bridge between your work and the customer's life.

Examples:
So you look professional and feel confident at work.
So your event feels special and memorable.
So your book looks credible and sells better.
So you feel clean and comfortable in your skin.
So you can get back to work and stay connected.

Now combine the three parts into one offer statement:

I make custom office shirts for working men so they look sharp and feel confident at work.
I bake celebration cakes for families so birthdays and weddings feel joyful and memorable.
I design book covers for self-publishing authors so their books look professional and sell with confidence.

That is your offer.

You will use it in your bio, your captions, your messages, and your ads if you run them later.

What you build in this chapter: a one-page marketing plan tied to one primary channel

The second thing you build is a one-page plan. Not a big document. One page.

The mistake I see often is chasing too many platforms at once.

Someone opens Facebook, Instagram, TikTok, YouTube, and WhatsApp in one week. They post once, get tired, then disappear. They conclude "online business doesn't work."

It works. They just had no focus.

Pick one primary channel for the next 30 days.

Your primary channel is where you will post consistently, learn what works, and build your first real audience.

Other channels can exist, but they are not the engine. They are just supporting roads.

How do you choose the primary channel?

Choose based on:
Where your customers already spend time
What kind of content you can produce consistently
What the platform rewards (photos, short video, long video, text)
How quickly you can respond to inquiries

For many small businesses, a strong combination is:
One content channel (like Instagram or TikTok)
One communication channel (like WhatsApp)

But keep one as the primary focus.

Your one-page plan (copy this)

1. Offer statement
   Write your one-sentence offer.
2. Target audience
   Write your primary customer group.
3. Primary channel
   Choose one.
4. Content types (pick 3)
   These are your weekly pillars.
   Examples:
   Process (behind the scenes)
   Product (what you sell)
   Proof (customer feedback)
   Education (tips and how-to)
   Story (why you started, what you believe)

Pick three so you stay consistent.

5. Posting rhythm
   Decide what you can maintain.
   Example:

3 posts a week + 5 stories
Or 4 short videos a week
Or 2 posts a week + daily replies and updates

Consistency beats intensity.

6. Call to action
   What do you want them to do?
   Message me to order
   Join my WhatsApp list
   Book an appointment
   Visit my website
   Call this number

Pick one main action so you do not confuse people.

7. Follow-up system
   What happens after they message you?
   You reply with pricing
   You share samples
   You confirm details
   You send payment info
   You confirm delivery

If you do not have a follow-up system, attention will leak and you will feel busy without selling.

8. Simple weekly metrics
   Track only what matters:
   Number of inquiries
   Number of orders
   Total sales
   Repeat customers
   Content posted (yes or no)

Do not drown in numbers. Track actions and outcomes.

That is your one-page plan.

Practice: define your offer, pick your main platform, write your first clear message

Now we do the work.

Practice 1: Define your offer in one sentence
Use this structure:

I help (who) get (result) by (what you sell).

Examples:
I help busy office workers look sharp by making custom office shirts.
I help families celebrate big moments by baking custom cakes.
I help authors publish with confidence by designing professional book covers.

Write yours. Keep it plain.

Practice 2: Pick your main platform for 30 days
Answer these questions:

Where do my customers already spend time?
Can I post here consistently without stress?
Can I show my product well here?
Can customers easily contact me from here?

Choose one. Commit for 30 days.

Practice 3: Write your first clear message
Your first message is not a poem. It is not an essay. It is clarity.

Here are three message templates you can use today.

Template A (Direct)
I make (product/service) for (who).
If you want (benefit), message me here and I'll share options and pricing.

Template B (Problem to solution)
If you struggle with (problem), I can help.

I offer (product/service) for (who) so you get (result).
Message me to order or ask questions.

Template C (Story-based)
I started (business) because (short reason).
Now I help (who) get (result) through (product/service).
If you want to try it, message me and I'll guide you.

Now write your first message and post it.

Do not wait for perfection.

A final word for this chapter
Digital marketing is not a trick. It is not manipulation. It is not "internet talk."

It is the discipline of showing up where people already are, communicating clearly, and building trust through proof and consistency.

If you are small, this is good news. It means you can compete without large capital. You can grow without renting the most expensive shop. You can build an audience before you build a building.

But you must do the work.

Define your offer.
Choose your primary channel.
Say your message clearly.
Follow up like a professional.
Track what matters.

If you do these things, you will feel the shift in your business. You will move from waiting to building.

And that is the beginning of entrepreneurship in the digital age.

Chapter Two: Understanding Target Audience

If Chapter One is about attention, then Chapter Two is about direction.

Attention without direction is expensive. You can post every day, reply to many people, and still feel broke. You can gain followers and still have no serious buyers. You can even go viral and still struggle to pay rent.

That happens when you talk to everyone.

Entrepreneurship forces one uncomfortable decision: I must choose my people.

Not because I hate others, but because I want my message to land. And for a message to land, it must be written for a specific mind, a specific need, and a specific wallet.

When I say "target audience," I do not mean a fancy marketing phrase. I mean the real human beings who will pay you, return, refer friends, and defend your brand when others criticize it.

This chapter will show you how I identify the ideal customer using basic market research and platform data, focusing on demographics and online behavior, then turning that into clearer messaging.

Why most small businesses stay stuck

A struggling business usually has one of these problems:

- The offer is unclear.
- The audience is unclear.
- The message is unclear.
- The follow-up is weak.
- The product is not good enough yet.

In this chapter, we fix the second and third problems: audience and message.

Because the fastest way to waste energy is to market to people who will never buy.

Some people like your post but will not pay.
Some people ask many questions but will not order.
Some people want discounts only.
Some people are not your customer, and that is fine.

Your job is not to convince everyone.

Your job is to find the right people, then speak to them so clearly that they feel you are reading their mind.

That is what "ideal customer" means.

What I teach: how I find the ideal customer (simple market research + platform data)

I start with two sources of truth:

- The market itself (what people already buy and talk about)
- My platform data (who interacts with my posts and how they behave)

Step 1: Start with your current buyers (even if they are few)

If you have sold to even five people, you already have clues.

I ask:

- Who bought from me without too much persuasion?
- Who paid fast and did not negotiate too much?
- Who was happy after delivery?
- Who came back again?
- Who referred someone?

That group is gold.

If you ignore them and chase strangers, you punish loyalty and reward noise.

Example with our teaching character:

Nyakor sells clothes. She notices something. Students love her designs but always want a cheaper price. Office workers order fewer pieces, but they pay fast and ask for quality and fitting. Brides order occasionally, but when they order, they spend more and bring friends.

Right there, Nyakor has three possible audiences.

If she tries to serve all three with the same message, her marketing becomes confused.

If she chooses one primary group for the next 30 days, her message becomes sharp.

Step 2: Observe the market where people already talk
I do not guess what people want. I look.

Where do I look?

- Comments under competitor pages (what people praise, complain about, ask)
- Reviews on marketplaces (what people love, what hurts them)
- Search suggestions in platforms (what people type)
- Local groups (what people ask repeatedly)
- Direct messages (the same questions again and again)

You do not need money for this research. You need attention and discipline.

Write down exact phrases people use.

People tell you their pain in their own words. Those words become your best marketing copy later.

Example:

If people keep asking:
"Do you deliver?"
"Do you do fitting?"
"How long does it take?"
"Is it original?"
"Can I pay on delivery?"
"Do you have plus sizes?"

Those are not "annoying questions."

Those are buying signals.

Step 3: Use platform data (even basic data is enough)
Most platforms show basic analytics:

- Age ranges
- Gender split
- Location
- Active hours
- Top posts (what got the most saves, shares, comments, clicks)

I do not worship numbers. I use them to make better decisions.

I look for patterns:

- What posts bring serious inquiries?
- What posts bring cheap talk only?
- When do my buyers come online?
- What content makes people save (saves often mean "I want this later")?
- What content makes people share (shares spread trust faster)?

If your best posts are educational tips, then your audience likes learning. Your messaging should include guidance, not only pricing.

If your best posts are before-and-after, then your audience wants proof. Your messaging should include results and testimonials.

If your best posts are short process videos, then your audience wants to see how it's made. Your messaging should highlight craftsmanship and quality control.

This is how online behavior shapes messaging.

Step 4: Match demographics to buying behavior (not stereotypes)
Demographics are useful, but they are not the full story.

Age and location tell me "who."
Behavior tells me "why they buy."

A 22-year-old student and a 22-year-old office intern might behave differently.
A 40-year-old mother and a 40-year-old manager might behave differently.

So I connect demographics to behavior:

- Who asks about price first?
- Who asks about durability and quality first?
- Who wants speed and convenience?
- Who wants style and uniqueness?
- Who wants trust and safety?

I do not judge. I just observe.

Because a business grows faster when it serves what people truly value.

What you build: the Ideal Customer Page
Now we build a single page that becomes your marketing compass.

Not a long document. One page you can read in two minutes before you write a post, design a flyer, or reply to messages.

Ideal Customer Page (copy and fill)

1) Name your ideal customer (give them a real identity)

- Name (example): "Mary the Office Professional"
- Age range:
- Location:
- Work/life situation:

This is not to pretend. It is to focus your mind.

2) What do they want right now?

- What outcome are they chasing?
- What problem are they trying to solve this month?
- What would make them feel proud after buying?

Example (office professional buying clothes):

- Wants to look sharp at work.
- Wants clothes that fit and last.
- Wants to stop wasting money on poor tailoring.

3) What do they fear or dislike?

- What have they tried that disappointed them?
- What makes them hesitate to pay?
- What would make them regret buying?

Examples:

- Fear of bad fitting.
- Fear of late delivery.
- Fear of fake quality photos.
- Fear of being ignored after payment.

If you know these fears, you can remove them in your message.

4) What makes them trust?
Trust is not built by claiming "best quality." Trust is built by proof and behavior.

Write:

- What kind of proof do they believe?
- What signals tell them you are serious?

Examples:

- Clear pricing ranges.
- Real customer photos.
- Short process videos.
- Consistent posting (not disappearing).
- Fast replies.
- A clear policy (delivery, refunds, adjustments).
- A visible location or delivery record.

5) What language do they use?

- Common phrases they type in messages:
- Words they use when they complain:
- Words they use when they praise:

Use their words in your captions and replies.

6) What do they do online?
This is the behavior part.

- What platform do they use most?
- What content do they save?
- What time are they active?
- Do they prefer video or photos?
- Do they message fast or watch quietly first?

7) What is the simplest message that will catch them?
Write a one sentence hook that speaks directly to them.

Examples:

- "Custom office shirts that fit well and last, made with clean finishing and delivered on time."
- "Wedding fittings without stress: clear timelines, clear pricing, and a perfect fit."

That is your Ideal Customer Page.

Keep it close. Use it daily.

What you also build: keywords and conversation topics

Keywords are not only for search engines. Keywords are also for human brains.

When you repeat the right phrases consistently, people remember you for something specific.

When your words are random, people forget you quickly.

Step 1: Build a short keyword list (10 to 20 phrases)
Use three types of keywords:

1. Product keywords (what you sell)
   Examples:

   - custom office shirts
   - wedding gown alterations
   - book cover design
   - birthday cake delivery
   - phone screen replacement

2. Problem keywords (what pain you solve)
   Examples:

   - clothes that don't fit
   - last-minute outfit
   - cheap tailoring issues
   - slow delivery

- poor finishing

3. Benefit keywords (what outcome they want)
   Examples:

- look professional
- confidence at work
- perfect fit
- durable fabric
- clean finishing
- fast turnaround

Your keyword list should match your offer and your ideal customer.

Step 2: Build conversation topics (the things you will post and talk about)
Conversation topics are your content fuel.

If you do not plan topics, you will wake up and post anything, then feel tired and confused.

Here are topic buckets that work in almost any business:

- Proof (customer feedback, before-and-after, results)
- Process (how it's made, behind the scenes, quality checks)
- Education (tips, mistakes to avoid, how to choose)
- Story (why I started, what I believe, what I learned)
- Pricing clarity (ranges, what affects price, what you get)
- Service clarity (delivery, timelines, policies)

Now connect topics to your ideal customer.

Example for "office professional":

- How to choose office fabric that lasts.
- Why fitting matters more than size.
- Three shirt mistakes that make you look cheaper.
- A simple weekly wardrobe plan for busy workers.

- Behind the scenes: finishing a collar properly.
- Customer story: from frustration to confidence.

When your topics match your customer's life, your posts stop being noise.

Practice: stop chasing everyone, choose the right people, speak directly

This practice is the turning point for many readers.

Because this is where you stop begging and start leading.

Practice 1: Choose your primary audience for the next 30 days

Pick one group.

Not forever. For now.

You can expand later.

But right now, you need focus.

Ask these questions:

- Who pays with less resistance?
- Who values what I do?
- Who can afford my pricing without begging?
- Who is most likely to return?
- Who is most likely to refer?

Choose the group that scores highest.

Write it down.

"I am building for ____."

Practice 2: Write three "direct-to-them" messages

Use your Ideal Customer Page to write messages that sound like you are speaking to one person.

Here are three templates.

Template A (Identity + desire)
If you are a (type of person) who wants (result), I can help.
I offer (product/service) so you get (benefit).
Message me for options and pricing.

Template B (Fear removal)
Many people fear (common fear).
Here is how I solve it: (proof or process).
If you want (result), message me and I'll guide you.

Template C (Proof-driven)
This is what I delivered this week: (result).
This is what the customer said: (short quote).
If you want the same outcome, message me.

Write three messages and post one this week.

Practice 3: Tighten your bio and headline
Your bio is your first sales pitch. Most bios are useless.

A strong bio answers:
Who do I help?
What do I deliver?
Where are you located or how do you serve?

Example:
Custom office shirts and fitting services for working professionals in Nairobi. Clean finishing, clear timelines. Orders via WhatsApp.

Simple. Clear. Actionable.

Practice 4: One week of targeted content (small but serious)
For the next 7 days, post only with your chosen audience in mind.

Post ideas:

- One proof post (customer feedback or result)

- One process post (behind the scenes)
- One education post (tip or mistake to avoid)
- One direct offer post (pricing range + how to order)

Then watch what happens in your messages.

Targeted content attracts targeted buyers.

Why smarter targeting beats wider targeting
Let me say this plainly.

If you target everyone, you compete on price.
If you target the right people, you compete on value.

If you target everyone, your message becomes vague.
If you target the right people, your message becomes sharp.

If you target everyone, you get noise.
If you target the right people, you get orders.

Wider is not always better.

Clear is better.

A short example you can learn from
Nyakor was posting dresses, shirts, suits, kids' clothes, and bridal gowns all in one week. Her page looked busy, but it was not building a strong signal. People could not tell what she stood for. Inquiries were random. Most messages were price questions.

She chose one group for 30 days: office professionals.

She adjusted her content:

- Workwear results.
- Shirt fitting process.
- Fabric tips.
- Clear timelines.
- Clear pricing range.

The audience changed.

Fewer messages, but better messages.
Fewer likes, but more serious inquiries.
Less noise, more sales.

That is the power of choosing.

Chapter Two summary (what you should have now)
By the end of this chapter, you should have:

- One Ideal Customer Page (filled and real)
- A short keyword list tied to your offer
- A list of conversation topics you can post weekly
- One chosen primary audience for the next 30 days
- Three direct messages written for that audience

If you do not do this work, your marketing will always feel like guessing.

If you do this work, your next chapter becomes easier, because branding and content become clear when your customer is clear.

In the next chapter, we will connect your offer and audience to the digital ecosystem, meaning how your platforms, content, and communication flow can work as one system instead of scattered effort.

Chapter Three: Navigating the Digital Ecosystem

In the first chapter, I taught you how digital marketing turns attention into growth. In the second chapter, I taught you how to choose the right people and speak to them clearly. Now we reach a point where many small businesses either become stable, or remain scattered.

This chapter is about building one working system.

Not a collection of apps.
Not random posting.
Not opening accounts everywhere.

A system.

When your business becomes digital, you are no longer only selling a product. You are managing a path. You are guiding a customer from discovery to trust, from trust to payment, from payment to delivery, and from delivery to repeat purchase.

If that path is broken, you will work hard and still lose money.

If that path is simple and connected, even a small shop can feel organized, professional, and ready to grow.

That is why I call it a digital ecosystem: the platforms, tools, and habits that work together as one machine.

What I teach: how I choose platforms and connect them into one working system

Let me begin with a mindset that has saved me years of confusion.

Your business must have a "home," and it must also have "roads."

Home is where your business truly lives.
Roads are where people discover you.

Many entrepreneurs build only roads. They post every day on social media, but they have no home base. If the platform changes rules, if their account is restricted, or if they get tired and disappear, the whole business collapses.

So I build it differently.

I build a digital home first, then I build roads that lead to it, then I build a follow-up habit that turns visitors into customers.

The five parts of a working system
A complete system has five connected parts:

Visibility
How people find you.

Trust
How they believe you are real and reliable.

Conversion
How they buy, meaning how they move from interest to payment.

Fulfillment
How you deliver what you promised.

Retention
How you keep them and bring them back.

If one part is missing, money leaks.

A page that gets many views but no orders has a conversion problem.
A business that gets orders but gets complaints has a fulfillment problem.
A business that sells once but never sees customers again has a retention problem.

This is why platform choice matters. Platforms are not decoration. They should strengthen these five parts.

How I choose platforms (the simple filter)
I use five questions to choose platforms, and I recommend you do the same:

Where is my target audience active?
Not where people talk the loudest, but where your buyers spend time.

What content can I produce consistently?
If you hate video, do not force short videos every day. If you can write well, use that strength.

How easy is contact and follow-up?
A platform that makes it hard for people to message you will slow your sales.

How does payment happen?
If your buyers prefer mobile money, build around that reality.

How does delivery happen?
If you deliver locally, build a local-first system. If you ship, build order tracking and clear policies.

Now let's talk about the most important idea in this chapter.

Your digital home vs rented space
Social media is rented space.

Your website, store page, and email list are closer to home.

I say "closer," because even a website can depend on hosting, and even email depends on providers. But the difference is control. A platform can reduce your reach overnight. A website and an email list are far more stable.

So I structure it like this:

Home base
A website or a store page where your offer is clear, your pricing is

explained, your proof is visible, and your contact options are obvious.

Supporting platforms
Social media platforms that send people to your home base, plus direct communication channels for fast sales.

You do not need everything. You need the right connections.

For many small businesses, this works well:

Home base: a simple website (even one page), or a store page.
Roads: one main social platform.
Direct sales: a messaging channel.
Long-term follow-up: an email list.

Let me name a few common tools so you can picture it:

A simple site with WordPress or a store built with Shopify can serve as home base.
For roads, many people use Instagram, Facebook, TikTok, or YouTube.
For direct sales, WhatsApp is powerful because it feels personal and fast.
For email, a tool like MailerLite can help you keep customers and build repeat business.
For search visibility, Google matters, especially for local buyers.

You will not use all of these at once. You will choose based on your target audience and capacity.

What you build: your Digital Home Map

A Digital Home Map is a simple picture of your system. You can draw it on paper.

It answers one question:

When a stranger meets my business today, what exact steps take them to purchase, receive delivery, and come back again?

Digital Home Map template
1) Home base
Choose one:
Website (simple, one page is fine)
Store page (simple catalog and order button)
Marketplace page (if that's where buyers already purchase)

2) Visibility roads
Choose one primary road:
Main social platform where you post consistently
Optional secondary road:
A second platform you use lightly, mostly repurposed content

3) Contact and conversion
Choose your main conversion path:
Messaging (fast, personal)
Order form (structured, reduces confusion)
Checkout (best for product businesses)

4) Payment
List your payment options:
Mobile money
Bank transfer
Card payment
Cash on delivery (only if safe and manageable)

5) Delivery and fulfillment
List your delivery method:
Customer pickup
Rider delivery
Courier shipping
Digital delivery (for services, ebooks, designs)

6) Follow-up and retention
Choose one method:
Email list for updates and repeat offers
Broadcast list for weekly updates
Customer care routine (check-in messages, loyalty offers)

That is the map.

When it is clear, your business feels simpler. When it is unclear, you feel busy and stressed.

A practical example (using the teaching story)
Nyakor sells office wear. Her map might look like this:

Home base: a one-page site showing her best products, pricing ranges, fitting schedule, and order steps.
Visibility road: Instagram as the primary platform.
Contact and conversion: WhatsApp for orders and fittings.
Payment: mobile money and bank transfer.
Delivery: local rider delivery, plus pickup option.
Follow-up: weekly WhatsApp broadcast with new designs and available slots.

Notice what is happening.

Everything connects.
Nothing is random.

That is the goal.

Connecting the system: website, social, email, payments, delivery

Now I will show you how I connect the parts so customers do not get lost.

Step 1: Make your home base do the heavy lifting
Your home base should answer the most common buyer questions without a long conversation.

At minimum, your home base should include:

Your offer statement
What you sell, who it is for, why it matters.

Proof
Customer photos, testimonials, results, examples.

Pricing guidance
Not necessarily exact prices for everything, but clear ranges and what affects price.

How to order
Step-by-step, simple.

Delivery information
Where you deliver, timelines, and any fees.

Contact buttons
WhatsApp button, email, phone, booking link.

If your home base is missing these, you will repeat yourself all day, and you will still lose buyers who do not want long chats.

Step 2: Turn social media into roads, not storage
Social media should push people to your next step.

Every post should lead somewhere:

Message me on WhatsApp to order.
Visit the link in bio to see options.
Join my email list for weekly updates.
Book your slot here.

If you only post and hope people magically buy, you are not guiding them. You are entertaining them.

Entertainment does not always pay.

Guidance pays.

Step 3: Build a simple follow-up mechanism
Many sales are not lost because the customer said no. They are lost because you failed to follow up.

People get distracted.
They run out of data.

They receive a call.
They forget.

So I build follow-up into the system.

Examples of follow-up that work:

A short reply script after inquiry:
"Thanks for reaching out. What are you looking for, and what is your budget range? I'll suggest the best options."

A reminder after they stop replying:
"Just checking in. Do you still want to order this week, or should I reserve your slot for next week?"

A confirmation after payment:
"Payment received. Here is your timeline, and I will update you at each stage."

A check-in after delivery:
"How is the fit and comfort? If you need a small adjustment, tell me."

This is how you turn one sale into trust.

Trust creates repeat business.

Step 4: Align payment and delivery with your audience reality

Many online business failures are not marketing failures. They are payment and delivery failures.

If your customers prefer mobile money, accept it.
If your customers need receipts for work reimbursement, provide them.
If your area has delivery challenges, create a clear pickup option.
If deliveries are delayed often, set expectations clearly and update customers proactively.

The more your system matches reality, the less stress you carry.

Visibility: SEO and consistent engagement

Now let's talk about visibility. Not only social visibility, but search visibility too.

People search for what they need when they are ready to buy.

That is why SEO matters.

SEO is simply making your business easy to find through search, and making your pages match what people are looking for.

You do not need to become a technical expert. You need a simple plan.

What you build: a simple SEO and content plan
Here is what I recommend for a small business.

1) Choose your keyword themes
Use the keywords you created in Chapter Two.

Pick 3 to 5 themes that match your offer and audience.

Examples for a tailor:
custom office shirts
workwear for professionals
fitting and alterations
quality fabric tips
style advice for office workers

Examples for a baker:
birthday cake delivery
wedding cake orders
cake pricing and sizes
cake design ideas
how to choose flavors

2) Create "answer content"
Answer content is content that solves questions people already ask.

If people ask:
"How much does it cost?"
"How long does it take?"
"Do you deliver?"
"What is the difference between these options?"

Make content that answers those questions.

This content works on social media and on a website.

3) Set up basic local search
If you serve a city or neighborhood, local search is a gold mine.

Set up a business profile, add accurate location, hours, photos, and encourage real reviews.

When people search "tailor near me" or "cake delivery Nairobi," you want to appear.

4) Use consistent naming
Use the same business name and contact across platforms.

Confusion kills trust.

5) Keep engagement steady
Search and social both reward consistency.

Consistency does not mean posting 5 times a day. It means staying visible with a rhythm you can sustain.

The strongest businesses online often win because they show up longer than everyone else.

Practice: choose platforms, set up the basics, and keep it consistent
Now we do the practical work.

Practice 1: Choose the platforms where your audience is active

Pick:
One home base.
One primary road.
One direct sales channel.
Optional: one retention channel.

Example choices:
Home base: one-page website.
Primary road: Instagram or Facebook.
Direct sales: WhatsApp.
Retention: email list.

Write your choices down.

Practice 2: Set up the basics (do this in one day)

Profile essentials
Clear profile photo or logo.
Clear offer statement in bio.
Clear location or service area.
Clear contact button or link.
Clear highlights or pinned posts showing proof, pricing, and ordering steps.

Home base essentials
A page that includes:
Offer
Proof
Pricing guidance
Order steps
Delivery info
Contact buttons

Conversion essentials
A reply script for inquiries.
A simple pricing sheet or standard message.
A clear timeline message.
A payment message.

Fulfillment essentials
A simple delivery method.
A basic policy:
What happens if delivery is late?
What happens if an adjustment is needed?
What happens if a customer cancels?

Policies protect trust.

Practice 3: Keep it consistent for 30 days (the simple discipline)
For the next 30 days:

Post on your primary road at a pace you can maintain.
Reply to messages within a set window, for example within 12 or 24 hours.
Track inquiries and orders weekly.
Do not change platforms every week.
Do not chase every trend.
Do not abandon the system because of a slow week.

If you want growth, you must stay long enough for people to trust you.

A simple weekly plan you can copy
Two proof posts
Customer results, testimonials, finished work.

One process post
Behind the scenes.

One education post
A tip that helps your audience.

Daily engagement
Short replies, comments, and stories.

This plan is small, but it works because it matches how people buy: they watch, they wait, they trust, then they act.

The point of the digital ecosystem

Let me end with the heart of this chapter.

You are not building a page.
You are building a path.

A path that takes a stranger from "Who is this?" to "I trust this person," to "I want this," to "I paid," to "I received it," to "I will come back."

That path is your ecosystem.

When your ecosystem is connected, your business becomes calmer. When your ecosystem is scattered, your business becomes stressful.

Choose your home base.
Choose your roads.
Connect contact, payment, and delivery.
Build visibility through SEO and consistency.
Stay steady for 30 days.

If you do this, the next part becomes easier, because branding and content become strong when the system behind them is strong.

Next, we move into Part Two, where we build your online brand so your presence looks professional, feels trustworthy, and speaks with one clear voice.

PART TWO: BUILDING YOUR ONLINE PRESENCE
Field Guide (Brand Assets)
A User's Guide to Photography for Your Online Business

Photography is not decoration.

In online business, photography is proof. It is the first handshake. It is the first moment of trust.

Most customers do not read long captions first. They look. They judge. They decide whether to stay or scroll.

So if your photos are unclear, dark, messy, inconsistent, or dishonest, customers leave before you even speak.

This field guide will show you how I use light, framing, and captions to sell without sounding desperate, and how I keep my feed visually consistent so my business looks serious.

I will make this practical. No expensive camera required. A phone is enough if you learn how to use it well.

1) The purpose of business photography
A business photo should do at least one of these jobs:

Show the product clearly
The customer must understand what it is, how it looks, and what makes it valuable.

Show proof
The photo should reduce doubt. It should feel real, not fake.

Show quality
The photo should highlight finishing, texture, and details.

Show context
Where does the product fit in life? What problem does it solve?

Show brand
Does the photo match the identity and feeling you want customers to associate with you?

If a photo does none of these, it may get likes, but it will not consistently get sales.

2) Light: the cheapest upgrade you can make
Light is the difference between "professional" and "cheap-looking."

Many people think they need a better camera. No. They need better light.

Use natural light first
The best free light is near a window or outside in shade.

Here is what I do:

Indoor window light
Stand near a window. Let the light fall on the product from the side. Avoid strong light from behind the product because it creates a silhouette and hides details.

Outdoor shade
Go outside, but stand in shade. Shade gives soft light. Direct sunlight creates harsh shadows and makes colors look wrong.

Best times for outdoor photos
Morning
Soft light, clean look.

Late afternoon
Soft light, warm look.

Avoid midday sun if possible.

The simple test for good light
If you can see fabric texture, stitching lines, cake details, or product edges clearly with your eyes, the camera will capture it better too.

If you struggle to see details with your eyes, the camera will struggle even more.

3) Background: remove clutter, increase trust
Clutter kills professionalism.

A messy background makes your product look cheaper. It also confuses the viewer because the eye does not know where to focus.

Choose a simple background
Good backgrounds:

Plain wall
Plain bedsheet
Wood table
Clean floor
Neutral cloth
Simple board

Bad backgrounds:

Dirty rooms
Random items behind product
Busy patterns that fight attention
Unmade beds with clothes
Crowded markets (unless the market itself is part of the brand story)

If your brand identity is "clean and professional," your background must match it.

If your brand identity is "warm and handmade," you can use natural textures like wood, simple cloth, or home settings, but still keep it controlled.

4) Framing: how to position the product so it sells
Framing is simply how you place the product and what you include in the photo.

A good frame makes the product obvious and desirable.

Use these four shot types (rotate them)
1) The hero shot
The product fills most of the frame.
The background is simple.
This is the main selling photo.

Example:
A shirt laid flat, clean, centered.
A cake on a clean table, centered.
A book cover mockup, centered.

2) The detail shot
Zoom in and show quality.

Example:
Stitching, collar, buttons, fabric texture.
Cake layers, frosting texture, design detail.
Design details in a cover, typography clarity.

3) The context shot
Show the product in real life.

Example:
A customer wearing the shirt.
A cake on a celebration table.
A book on a desk with a reader's hand nearby.

Context helps customers imagine themselves with the product.

4) The process shot
Show behind the scenes.

Example:
Measuring, cutting, sewing, packaging.
Mixing batter, decorating, boxing.
Sketching design, editing layout, presenting drafts.

Process photos build trust because they show effort and authenticity.

Keep your horizon straight
A tilted photo makes your page look careless.

Most phones allow you to turn on grid lines. Turn them on. Align your product with the grid.

Leave breathing space
Do not crop too tightly all the time.

Let the product breathe so it looks premium.

5) Consistency: the hidden power of a strong feed
Many pages fail not because the products are bad, but because the feed looks random.

Inconsistency creates doubt.

Consistency creates familiarity.

Familiarity creates trust.

Trust creates sales.

How I keep my feed consistent
I choose:

A consistent light style:
Mostly natural light.

A consistent background style:
Mostly plain or neutral.

A consistent angle style:
Mostly straight-on or slightly angled.

A consistent editing style:
Same brightness and contrast style every time.

A consistent posting rhythm:
Even if it is only 3 times a week, I keep it.

When a customer scrolls my page, they should feel one business speaking, not many different moods.

6) Editing: improve without lying
Editing is good, but dishonest editing destroys trust.

If you change colors too much, customers will feel cheated.

If you smooth everything, your product looks fake.

My rule is simple:

Edit to match real life, not to invent a new reality.

Basic edits that help
Increase brightness slightly if the photo is dark.
Increase contrast slightly so details are clearer.
Adjust warmth if the color looks too cold.
Crop to remove distractions.
Sharpen slightly to show texture.

Avoid heavy filters that change the true product color.

7) Phone camera settings that actually matter
You do not need to become technical. But a few settings help.

Clean your lens
This sounds small, but it makes a big difference.

A dirty lens creates a soft, dull photo.

Use the back camera
Back camera is usually higher quality than selfie camera.

Tap to focus
Tap on the product so the camera focuses where it matters.

Avoid digital zoom
Digital zoom reduces quality. Instead, move closer to the product.

Use portrait mode carefully

Portrait mode can look premium, but it can also cut edges badly if the phone struggles.

Use it when:
The product is clearly separated from the background.

Avoid it when:
The product has messy edges or blended background, like detailed hair, lace, or complex shapes.

8) What to photograph (so you never run out of content)

Many business owners say, "I don't know what to post."

That is usually because they think content is only "finished products."

No.

You can photograph:

Finished product (hero shot)
Close-up details
Packaging
Before-and-after
Customer collection or pickup
Workstation (clean)
Tools of the trade
Fabric selection
Ingredient selection
Quality check moment
Delivery moment (if safe)
Testimonials screenshot (with permission)
My hands working (process)
Small mistakes and how I fixed them (very powerful)
Comparison of options (fabric types, sizes, flavors, etc.)

This gives you endless content without forcing creativity.

9) Captions that sell without sounding desperate

Many captions fail because they either:

Sound like begging:
"Please support my business"
"Help me grow"
"Share my post"
"Kindly buy"

Or they sound like noise:
Long words, unclear message, no call to action.

A strong caption does three things:

Speaks to the customer.
Shows value or proof.
Gives one clear next step.

My caption structure (simple and repeatable)

Line 1: Hook
Speak directly to the customer's desire or problem.

Examples:
Work shirts should fit well, not punish you all day.
A birthday cake should look beautiful and taste even better.
Your book cover is the first impression of your work.

Lines 2–4: Value or story
What you did, why it matters, what makes it different.

Examples:
I make custom office shirts with clean finishing and comfortable fit, designed for long workdays.
This cake was made for a child's 7th birthday, with flavor options and a design the family requested.
I design covers that look professional, match your genre, and help your book sell with confidence.

Line 5: Proof
Short evidence.

Examples:
Delivered in 3 days with two fittings.
Freshly baked and delivered on time.
Draft delivered in 48 hours with revisions included.

Last line: Call to action
One action.

Examples:
Message me to order and I'll share options and pricing.
Book your slot this week via WhatsApp.
Send your title and genre and I'll guide you.

That is it.

No begging. No desperation. Just clarity.

10) Pricing and photography: show value, not cheapness

If you only post cheap prices, you attract bargain hunters only.

If you show value, you attract serious buyers.

Photography helps you show value.

Show stitching close-ups.
Show packaging.
Show clean finishing.
Show process.
Show consistency.

These photos justify your price without arguing.

11) Proof photos: how to use customers ethically and effectively

Customer photos are powerful, but they require respect.

Rules I follow:

Ask permission before posting.
Blur faces if needed.
Avoid posting private details.
Respect modesty and dignity.
Do not embarrass customers.

Even better:
Let the customer send you a photo they feel comfortable sharing.

Proof should build trust, not create conflict.

12) A simple weekly photography plan

Here is a plan you can follow without stress.

Every week, capture:

Two hero shots (finished product)
Two detail shots (quality close-ups)
Two process shots (behind the scenes)
One context shot (product in real life)
One proof element (testimonial or customer feedback)

That gives you 8 pieces of content.

You can post 3 or 4 and keep the rest for later.

Consistency becomes easy when you plan like this.

13) Quick photography checklist (use before posting)

Light is clean and bright.
Background is simple.
Product is the focus.
Photo is not blurry.
Horizon is straight.
Color looks true.
Crop removes distractions.

Caption is clear and matches brand voice.
Call to action is one step only.

14) The deeper lesson behind photography

A strong feed is not about impressing people.

It is about reducing doubt.

Every photo either increases trust or increases doubt.

When you treat photography as part of your business system, you stop posting randomly. You start building a presence that feels stable, professional, and worth paying for.

And when customers trust you, marketing becomes easier.

Because you no longer chase attention.

Attention begins to come to you.

Next, we move to Chapter Five: Creating Engaging Content, where I will show you how to build a simple content system that supports your brand, attracts the right audience, and drives consistent sales without burning out.

PART TWO: BUILDING YOUR ONLINE PRESENCE
Chapter Five: Creating Engaging Content

Most people think content is for influencers.

That is the first misunderstanding.

Content is not for fame. Content is for trust.

When I run an online business, I do not post to entertain strangers. I post to guide potential customers from uncertainty to confidence. I post so that when a person is ready to buy, they already feel like they know me, they trust my work, and they understand what to do next.

If you only "post products," you will often face these problems:

People ask the same questions again and again.
People doubt your quality.
People compare you to the cheapest seller.
People negotiate aggressively.
People disappear after inquiry.
People say, "I will come back," and never come back.

Engaging content solves these problems because it builds familiarity and proof before the customer even sends a message.

In this chapter, I teach how I move from "posting products" to publishing content that builds trust, shows process, and pulls customers into the story behind the product.

And I will help you build a content rhythm that you can maintain without burnout.

1) The real purpose of content for business
Business content has four jobs:

Visibility
To help the right people discover you.

Trust
To reduce doubt and show proof.

Education
To remove confusion and answer questions.

Conversion
To guide people to the next step: message, order, book, pay.

If your content is missing any of these, you will feel busy but not grow.

Likes are not the goal. Sales and repeat customers are the goal. Content supports those goals.

2) The shift: from posting products to publishing a trust-building feed

Posting products is easy:

Here is the shirt.
Here is the cake.
Here is the cover design.
Buy it.

But customers rarely buy from a stranger just because they saw a product.

They buy because they trust:

They trust the quality.
They trust the delivery.
They trust the communication.
They trust the seller will not vanish after payment.

So I publish content that shows those truths.

That is why I focus on three kinds of content:

Behind-the-scenes
Shows the process and effort. Builds credibility.

Customer story
Shows results and real life impact. Builds proof.

Educational content
Shows expertise and care. Builds authority.

If you publish these consistently, your page becomes a living showroom and a trust machine.

3) What you build: a content rhythm you can keep
A content rhythm is a weekly plan that fits your life.

If your plan is too intense, you will quit.
If your plan is too weak, you will remain invisible.

So I build a rhythm that is realistic and repeatable.

Step 1: Choose weekly themes (simple, not complicated)
Weekly themes keep you focused.

You can choose themes based on:
Product categories
Customer needs
Your brand pillars
Seasonal demand

Here are examples.

For a tailor:
Week theme options:
Workwear week
Fitting and finishing week
Fabric education week

Customer spotlight week
Wedding season week

For a baker:
Flavor week
Design week
Delivery and packaging week
Celebration story week
Pricing clarity week

For a service provider:
Process week
Client story week
Tips week
Tools week
Results week

You do not need a new theme every day. One theme per week is enough.

The theme helps you create three posts that feel connected, not random.

Step 2: Choose reusable post types (this stops content stress)

Many people run out of ideas because they think every post must be unique.

I do the opposite.

I use reusable post types.

A post type is a repeatable structure that you can apply to different products every week.

Here are post types that work in almost any business.

Proof posts:
Before-and-after

Customer feedback screenshot
Finished product with result story
Repeat customer highlight

Process posts:
Time-lapse of making
Step-by-step carousel
Tools and materials
Quality check moment
Packaging and delivery preparation

Education posts:
Mistakes to avoid
How to choose options (fabric, size, flavor, design)
Pricing explanation (what affects cost)
Care tips (how to wash, store, maintain)
Frequently asked questions

Offer posts:
What I offer this week
Available slots
Limited batch
Order steps explained clearly

Story posts:
Why I started
What I learned
A challenge I overcame
A behind-the-scenes lesson

Now, choose 5 post types and keep them as your "content toolkit."

When you have a toolkit, you never feel stuck.

Step 3: Build a simple calendar (the smallest system that works)

A calendar does not need to be complicated.

Here is a simple weekly calendar you can copy:

Monday: educational post (tip or mistake to avoid)
Wednesday: behind-the-scenes post (process)
Friday: customer story post (proof)
Weekend: optional offer post (available slots or weekly summary)

This is four posts, but you can start with three if needed.

The goal is rhythm, not perfection.

4) What you build: a system for customer photos and testimonials

Customer photos and testimonials are not random gifts. They are assets. If you collect them correctly, they become the strongest marketing tool you own.

But most small businesses collect them poorly, or never collect them at all.

So I create a simple system.

Step 1: Ask at the right time

The best time to ask is after delivery, when the customer is happy.

Not before.
Not when they are stressed.
Not when you are still fixing something.

Right after a good result, ask politely.

Example message:
Thanks again for your order. If you're happy with it, can you share a quick photo or a short note about your experience? It helps people trust my work.

Simple. Respectful.

Step 2: Make it easy for the customer

Many customers do not write testimonials because they do not know what to say.

So I guide them.

Give them 2 or 3 questions:
What did you order?
What did you like most?
Would you recommend it?

Or give them a template:
I ordered _____.
What I loved was _____.
I recommend _____.

This makes it easy.

Step 3: Organize your proof assets
If you keep testimonials scattered in chat, you will lose them.

So I organize them in a simple way:

One folder for customer photos.
One folder for testimonials screenshots.
One document or note with short "best quotes."

Even on a phone, you can do this.

This turns proof into a library you can use anytime.

Step 4: Use proof ethically
Ask permission.
Respect privacy.
Blur faces if needed.
Do not post sensitive information.

Trust is the currency. Never damage it for content.

5) The three content engines that build trust
Now let's go deeper into the three posts you must publish each week.

A) Behind-the-scenes content (process builds credibility)

Behind-the-scenes content is powerful because it shows effort.

It tells the customer:
This person is not guessing.
This person has skill.
This person is careful.

Behind-the-scenes content can be simple:

Measuring tape and fabric selection
Mixing ingredients and decorating
Sketching and revising designs
Packaging and labeling
Quality check moment

The point is not to show everything.
The point is to show that you have standards.

Behind-the-scenes content reduces price negotiation because customers see why your price is what it is.

B) Customer story content (results build proof)

A customer story is more than a photo.

It is a small narrative that shows transformation.

Structure it like this:

Who is the customer (in general, not full private details)
What did they want
What did you deliver
What was the result
What did they say

Example:
A working professional needed two office shirts within four days for a new job. We chose a durable fabric, did one fitting, and

delivered on time. His feedback was that the fit felt comfortable all day and the finishing looked premium.

That is a customer story.

It sells without shouting.

C) Educational content (teaching builds authority)
Educational content answers real questions.

It reduces confusion and builds trust.

Examples:
How to choose fabric that lasts
Why fitting matters more than size
How to store a cake properly
How to choose a book cover style for your genre
What affects pricing and timelines

When you teach, customers assume you know what you are doing.

They also feel respected, because you are not treating them like money only.

6) The content tone: engaging without sounding desperate
This matters a lot.

Desperation in content pushes customers away.

It makes them think:
This person is struggling, so I can negotiate hard.
This person will accept anything.
This person will not deliver properly.

So I never write like a beggar.

I write like a professional.

Professional content feels like this:

Clear.
Confident.
Helpful.
Respectful.
Direct.

No begging.
No emotional manipulation.
No fake urgency every day.

Urgency can exist, but it must be true:
Only two slots left this week.
Only five cakes available for Saturday.
Orders close by Thursday.

Truth builds trust.

7) What engaging content looks like in practice

Here are examples of engaging content ideas you can rotate.

Educational post ideas:
Three mistakes people make when buying work shirts
How to choose the right size when ordering online
Why cheap stitching fails quickly
How to plan your cake order to avoid stress
How to judge a professional book cover

Behind-the-scenes ideas:
Cutting fabric for a clean collar finish
Mixing and decorating a cake from start to finish
Packaging an order for safe delivery
Testing colors and typography for a cover design
Preparing a product batch

Customer story ideas:
A client story with a simple result description
A testimonial screenshot with a short caption

Before-and-after photo with permission
Repeat customer appreciation post

Offer post ideas:
This week's available slots
New designs ready
Seasonal offer
Bundle options

8) Practice: your weekly content discipline
Here is the practice you must do.

Every week, publish:

One behind-the-scenes piece.
One customer story.
One educational post.

That is it.

If you do that for 12 weeks, your business will look different online.

You will have:
More proof.
More trust.
More clarity.
More sales conversations.
Better customers.

Now let me make it even easier.

Your weekly checklist (copy)
Behind-the-scenes post:
What part of my process will I show this week?
What simple caption will explain why it matters?
What is the call to action?

Customer story post:
Which customer experience can I share this week?
Do I have permission to share a photo or quote?
What result will I highlight?
What is the call to action?

Educational post:
What common question can I answer this week?
What tip can I give in simple language?
What mistake can I help them avoid?
What is the call to action?

Then schedule it.

9) How to avoid burnout while posting consistently
Consistency does not mean creating new content every day.

Here is how I avoid burnout:

I batch content:
One day, I take 10 photos.
One day, I write captions for 4 posts.
One day, I collect testimonials and organize them.

I repurpose content:
A behind-the-scenes video becomes:
A short clip.
A still photo post.
A story.
A before-and-after comparison.

I use templates:
Same caption structure.
Same post types.
Same weekly rhythm.

I keep it simple:
Three posts a week can build a strong business.

Burnout comes from trying to act like a big company with a small team.

You do not need that.

You need discipline and clarity.

Chapter Five summary (what you should have now)

By the end of this chapter, you should have:

A weekly content rhythm you can keep.
Reusable post types you can repeat without stress.
A simple calendar.
A system for customer photos and testimonials.
A weekly practice:
One behind-the-scenes piece.
One customer story.
One educational post.

If you do this, your page will stop looking like a random catalog.

It will become a story, a showroom, and a trust-building machine.

Next, we move to Chapter Six: The Art of Storytelling, where I will show you how to turn ordinary business moments into narratives that people remember, share, and buy from.

PART TWO: BUILDING YOUR ONLINE PRESENCE
Chapter Six: The Art of Storytelling

If you want to understand why some small businesses grow fast while others remain invisible, look at one thing: memory.

People buy what they remember.

They remember what touches them.
They remember what helps them.
They remember what makes them feel something real.

That is why storytelling is not decoration. It is a business tool. It is how I turn ordinary work into something customers connect with.

When I say "storytelling," I do not mean fiction. I mean meaning.

I mean the way I explain my work so customers feel why it matters, not just how much it costs.

A business without story becomes a commodity.
A commodity competes on price.
Price competition is a race to the bottom.

A business with story becomes a choice.
A choice earns loyalty.
Loyalty builds stability.

This chapter teaches you how I turn business into narrative, so customers feel meaning, not just price. Every stitch, pattern, and product becomes a message people remember.

And I will give you a toolkit you can use weekly, plus a story bank you keep adding to for the rest of your business life.

1) Why storytelling makes customers pay more and complain less

Let me be direct.

Customers are not always rational.

They do not buy only with logic. They buy with emotion, identity, and trust, then they justify it with logic later.

Storytelling feeds that human reality.

When a customer understands the story behind your product, three things happen:

They see value beyond the physical item.
They trust your standards and your intention.
They feel connected, and connection reduces aggressive negotiation.

That is why storytelling can actually increase your price power without you arguing.

If you tell your story well, the customer stops asking only:
"How much?"

They start asking:
"How do I order?"
"When can I get it?"
"Can you do one for me too?"

That is the shift.

2) Storytelling is not long writing. It is clear meaning.

Many business owners avoid storytelling because they think it means writing long paragraphs.

No.

A good business story can be:

One sentence in a caption.
A short voice note to a customer.
A small paragraph on a product page.
A 30-second video explaining what you did and why.

Storytelling is simply this:

A human situation + a problem + your work + a result.

That structure alone can change your marketing.

3) What you build: the storytelling toolkit
In this chapter, you build three story types:

Origin story
Product story
Customer transformation story

When you master these three, you will never run out of meaningful content.

A) Origin story (why I started and what I stand for)
Your origin story answers:

Why did I start?
What problem did I see?
What values do I hold?
What promise do I keep?

Most people write their origin story like a CV.

That is boring.

A strong origin story is not about how educated you are. It is about why you care.

Here are the building blocks:

1. The moment of starting
   What pushed you into this business?
2. The frustration or need you noticed
   What made you say, "This must be done better"?
3. The learning and discipline
   What did you learn by doing, failing, and improving?
4. The promise you now offer customers
   What can they trust you for?

Example (tailor):
I started because I watched too many people waste money on clothes that never fit well. I saw how a poor fit can steal confidence. I began sewing and measuring with one focus: make workwear that feels right, lasts, and looks clean. Today, I keep my promise through careful fitting, honest timelines, and clean finishing.

That is an origin story.

It is short, but it carries meaning.

B) Product story (why this product exists and what it says)

A product story answers:

Who is it for?
What problem does it solve?
What makes it different?
What result does it create?

A product story is where you turn "an item" into "a message."

Every stitch becomes a message:
I care about detail.
I care about durability.
I care about comfort.
I care about confidence.

Here is the product story structure I use:

The situation:
Who needs this and why?

The design decision:
What choices did I make and why?

The quality signal:
What detail shows standards?

The result:
What does the customer experience?

Example:
This office shirt is designed for long workdays. I chose a durable fabric that holds shape and stays comfortable. The collar is reinforced so it remains sharp after many washes, and the stitching is clean so the shirt looks premium up close. The result is simple: you walk into your day feeling confident.

That is a product story.

It sells without begging.

C) Customer transformation story (the real proof narrative)

This is the strongest story you can tell.

A customer transformation story answers:

Who was the customer (in general)?
What did they want?
What problem were they facing?
What did you deliver?
What changed for them?

Transformation does not always mean a big life change. It can be small, but meaningful:

From stress to relief.
From embarrassment to confidence.
From confusion to clarity.
From delay to reliability.
From cheapness to quality.

Here is the structure I use:

Before:
What was happening?

During:
What did I do?

After:
What changed?

Example:
A young man was starting a new job and needed office shirts fast. He had bought ready-made shirts before, but the fit always felt wrong and the stitching failed quickly. We measured him, did one fitting, and delivered two shirts with clean finishing in three days. When he wore them, he said he felt comfortable the whole day and looked sharp in meetings.

That is transformation.

It becomes proof plus story.

4) The story bank: your endless content library
A story bank is a simple habit.

It is where you store story raw material so you never run out.

Most people lose story because they do not record it.

They experience good moments, solve problems, deliver value, and then forget. Weeks later, they struggle to "think of something to post."

So I build a story bank.

What goes into the story bank
The best stories come from these places:

Customer questions
Customer problems you solved
Behind-the-scenes moments
Mistakes and how you fixed them
Small wins
Unexpected challenges
Meaningful customer feedback
Design decisions and why you chose them
Time pressure moments and how you delivered
Quality checks and standards

These are your stories.

Not fancy words. Real moments.

How I capture stories (simple method)
I keep a note on my phone titled: Story Bank.

Every time something happens, I write one line:

Customer wanted ____.
Customer feared ____.
I solved it by ____.
Result was ____.

Or:

Today I learned ____ about fabric, delivery, quality, customers.

Or:

A mistake happened: ____.
I fixed it by ____.
Lesson: ____.

Five lines are enough.

If you do this daily, you will have 50 stories in a month.

That is content for the whole year.

5) Turning story into content: simple formats

Now that you have the toolkit, let's make it usable.

Here are formats you can use on social media or product pages:

Short caption story (4 to 7 lines)
Carousel story (slide 1 hook, slide 2 problem, slide 3 process, slide 4 result)
Short video story (30 to 60 seconds)
Product page story paragraph
Customer testimonial with story context

Storytelling is flexible. The goal is meaning, not length.

6) The discipline: meaning without manipulation

Storytelling must be honest.

Online is full of exaggeration. If you lie, you may get quick sales, but you will lose long-term trust.

My rules:

I do not invent customer results.
I do not fake urgency.
I do not use sadness to manipulate.
I do not promise what I cannot deliver.

Truth is the best marketing strategy because it builds a stable reputation.

7) Practice: write one short brand story and pair it with one product post

Now we do the work.

Your practice has two outputs:

One brand story.
One product page or social post using that story.

Step 1: Write your short brand story (use this template)
Template:

I started ____ because ____.
I noticed ____.
I learned ____ through experience.
Today, I help ____ by ____.
My promise is ____.

Now write it in your voice. Keep it under 120 words.

Example format:
I started this tailoring work because I watched people waste money on clothes that never fit well. I noticed how a poor fit steals confidence, especially for working professionals. Over time, I learned that real quality is not only fabric, it is measurement, finishing, and honest timelines. Today, I help office workers dress with confidence through custom workwear that fits and lasts. My promise is clean finishing, clear communication, and delivery you can trust.

That is your brand story.

Step 2: Pair it with a product post (use this structure)
Post structure:

Hook (one line)
Brand story (short)
Product story (one paragraph)
Call to action (one line)

Example:
Hook: Workwear should help you feel confident, not uncomfortable.

Brand story: I started tailoring because I saw too many people buy clothes that never fit well. I wanted to build workwear that feels right and lasts.
Product story: This shirt is made with durable fabric, reinforced collar finishing, and clean stitching designed for long workdays. The fit is shaped to comfort, not just appearance.
Call to action: Message me to order and I'll share options, pricing, and timelines.

That is a selling story.

Not begging. Not shouting. Just meaning.

8) Quick checklist for story-based content
Before you post, ask:

Is the story true?
Is the message clear?
Does it show value or proof?
Does it connect to the customer's life?
Is the call to action one step?

If yes, publish it.

Chapter Six summary (what you should have now)
By the end of this chapter, you now have:

A storytelling toolkit:
Origin story, product story, customer transformation story.

A story bank habit:
A place to store story raw material every day.

A practice you can repeat weekly:
Write one short brand story and pair it with one product page or social post.

If you do this consistently, your business stops being "another seller."

It becomes a voice.

And people buy from voices they remember.

Next, we move to Part Three: Engaging Your Audience, where we will use social media, mobile marketing, and customer relationships to turn your growing attention and trust into consistent sales and repeat customers.

PART THREE: ENGAGING YOUR AUDIENCE
Chapter Seven: Social Media Mastery

Social media can either become your loudest distraction or your strongest business tool.

The difference is not talent. It is intention.

Most people treat social media like a lottery. They post, hope the algorithm is kind, and feel offended when nothing happens. Or they post too much, burn out, disappear, and return weeks later with the same confusion.

That approach creates noise.

Noise is activity without results.

I use social media differently. I use it to build community, not noise. That means I do not treat followers like numbers. I treat them like people. I show up with consistency, I communicate clearly, and I invite them into a journey they can recognize and trust.

In this chapter, I will show you how I do that using engagement habits, collaborations, and customer-driven content. Then I will help you build a platform plan and a simple engagement schedule you can follow without stress.

And finally, we will practice the daily discipline that turns social media into sales and loyalty.

1) What "social media mastery" really means
Social media mastery is not:

Posting every day without a plan
Going viral once
Having a big follower count
Copying trends you do not understand

Social media mastery is:

Consistent visibility to the right people
Clear messaging that matches your offer and audience
Community habits that build trust
A steady flow of inquiries and repeat buyers
A brand presence that feels stable and professional

I measure mastery by outcomes, not likes.

Outcomes:
More serious inquiries
Higher trust
Better customers
Repeat sales
Referrals
Stronger reputation

If your activity does not produce those outcomes, it is noise.

2) The mindset shift: I am not competing for attention, I am building trust
When you stop chasing the crowd, your business becomes calmer.

A crowd is unstable. They love you today and forget you tomorrow.

A community is stable. They remember you, support you, and come back.

Community is built through repeated positive contact.

That is why engagement matters more than popularity.

Your goal is not to impress strangers.
Your goal is to build a relationship with the right audience.

And the fastest relationship builder online is not content alone.

It is interaction.

3) The three pillars of social media mastery

If you remember nothing else from this chapter, remember these three pillars:

Content
What you publish and what it teaches people about you.

Engagement
How you interact, respond, and build relationships.

Consistency
How long you stay visible with the same message and standards.

Content attracts.
Engagement converts.
Consistency compounds.

Most people only post.
Few people engage well.
That is why most pages do not grow into real businesses.

4) What I teach: using social platforms to build community, not noise

Let's break down the three areas I promised: engagement habits, collaborations, and customer-driven content.

A) Engagement habits (the daily actions that build trust)

Engagement is not begging for likes.

Engagement is conversation that helps people feel seen.

Here are the engagement habits I use.

Habit 1: Reply fast, even if the reply is short
Speed is a trust signal.

When customers message you and you reply two days later, they assume:

You are not serious.
You are disorganized.
You might delay delivery too.
You might disappear after payment.

A fast reply does not need to be a long reply.

A fast reply can be:
Thanks for reaching out. What are you looking for and when do you need it?

That one sentence builds trust.

Even if you cannot solve everything immediately, reply to acknowledge the person and promise a next step.

Habit 2: Ask good questions (questions guide customers to buy)
Most sellers only answer questions. They do not ask questions.

But the seller who asks good questions leads the conversation.

Examples of good questions:

What is the occasion?
When do you need it?
What is your budget range?
Do you prefer comfort or a tight fit?
Which style do you like more, A or B?
Have you ordered something like this before?

These questions do two things:
They show professionalism.
They help you sell the right thing.

They also reduce misunderstandings, which reduces complaints.

Habit 3: Comment where your customers already are

Many business owners wait for customers to come to them.

I go where customers are already active.

This does not mean spamming people. It means being present.

If your customers are in local groups, comment helpfully.
If your customers follow certain pages, interact with those discussions.
If your audience watches certain creators, engage respectfully.

Your comments become small advertisements, but they feel human because they are part of a conversation.

Habit 4: Use stories or short updates to stay visible daily

You do not need to publish a full post every day.

But you should stay visible.

Short updates can be:

Behind-the-scenes clip
Packaging moment
Quick tip
Customer pickup
Availability update

This keeps your community warm.

A cold page feels abandoned.
A warm page feels alive.

Habit 5: Set boundaries so community stays healthy
Community is not chaos.

If you allow rude behavior, scammers, or disrespectful bargaining to dominate, your serious customers will leave quietly.

So I set boundaries:

Clear pricing and process
Clear rules in groups or broadcasts
Respectful communication tone
No harmful debates on business pages

A healthy community protects your brand.

B) Collaborations (borrow trust, multiply reach)
If you want to grow faster, do not grow alone.

Collaboration is one of the smartest ways to gain trust because it borrows someone else's credibility.

But it must be strategic.

I collaborate with:

Businesses that serve the same audience but do not compete directly
People who share similar values and standards
Creators whose audience matches my ideal customer

Examples:

A tailor collaborates with a shoe seller, a barber, a photographer, or a men's grooming brand.
A baker collaborates with an event planner, decorator, florist, or party supply shop.
A book cover designer collaborates with editors, writers, printers, or marketing coaches.

The goal is not "let's post together for fun."
The goal is shared audience and shared trust.

Types of collaborations that work
Feature swap:
I feature your business, you feature mine.

Bundle offer:
Customer buys X, gets Y.

Behind-the-scenes collaboration:
Show how the service combination creates a better result.

Referral partnership:
We send customers to each other with a clear process.

Live session or Q&A:
Answer common questions together.

The key is alignment.

If you collaborate with low-quality sellers, their bad reputation can touch you too.

So choose carefully.

C) Customer-driven content (turn buyers into marketing)
The strongest content is not what you say about yourself.
It is what customers show and say about you.

Customer-driven content includes:

Customer photos
Testimonials
Before-and-after
Customer stories
Repeat customer appreciation
User-generated content (customers posting your product and tagging you)

This content builds trust faster than any sales caption.

Why?

Because it feels real.

How I make customer-driven content consistent
I do not wait for it to happen randomly.

I build a routine:

After delivery, I ask for a photo or short feedback.
I keep a proof folder.
Every week, I share at least one customer-driven post.
I thank customers publicly and respectfully.
I make customers feel like part of the journey.

When customers feel valued, they share more.

Sharing is free marketing, but it must be earned through good service.

5) What you build: a platform plan
Now we move from ideas to structure.

A platform plan is a simple written plan that answers:

What I post
How often
Why it matters

This prevents burnout, inconsistency, and random posting.

Step 1: Choose your primary platform
Pick one platform as your main stage.

This should be where your audience already is and where you can show your work well.

Your secondary platforms can exist, but the primary platform gets your best energy.

Step 2: Define your content mix
Your content mix is the balance of post types you will publish.

Here is a strong mix that works for most businesses:

30% proof (customer stories, testimonials, results)
30% process (behind the scenes, quality checks, making)
30% education (tips, mistakes, how to choose)
10% direct offer (availability, pricing ranges, order steps)

This mix builds trust and still sells.

If you do 80% offers, people get tired.
If you do 80% entertainment, you get followers but no buyers.
This mix keeps the page grounded in business.

Step 3: Choose a posting rhythm you can sustain
Start simple.

Three posts per week is enough if you engage daily.

Example rhythm:
Monday: educational post
Wednesday: behind-the-scenes process post
Friday: customer story or proof post
Weekend: optional offer post

If you can do four posts, add an offer post on Saturday.

The key is to repeat the rhythm long enough for your audience to learn your pattern.

People trust patterns.

Step 4: Define the purpose of each post
Every post must have a reason.

Ask:
What is this post trying to achieve?

Possible purposes:
Build trust
Show quality
Answer a common question
Show proof
Invite inquiries
Remind people you exist
Strengthen community

When you publish with purpose, your page becomes a system, not an accident.

6) What you build: a simple engagement schedule
This is the part many people ignore.

But engagement is where business is built.

Here is a simple schedule you can copy.

Daily engagement schedule (30 to 45 minutes total)
Morning (10 minutes):
Reply to messages and comments.
Like and respond to any serious inquiries.

Afternoon (10 minutes):
Comment on 5 to 10 posts where your audience is active (groups, local pages, related creators).
Do not spam. Add value.

Evening (10 to 25 minutes):
Post a story update or short status (if you have one).
Check messages again.
Follow up with 2 to 5 warm leads who went quiet.

That is it.

You do not need to spend your whole day online.

But you must show up consistently.

Weekly engagement schedule (one deeper session)
Once a week, do one of these:

A Q&A post
A short live session
A poll asking what customers want
A collaboration feature
A customer spotlight post
A behind-the-scenes story series

This keeps community active.

7) Practice: reply fast, ask good questions, feature customers, invite them into the journey
Now we do the discipline that turns social media into community.

Practice 1: Reply fast with a professional structure
Create three saved replies:

Inquiry reply:
Thanks for reaching out. What are you looking for and when do you need it?

Pricing reply:
Pricing depends on size and design. Share what you want and your budget range, and I'll recommend the best option.

Timeline reply:
If we confirm today, delivery is in ___ days. I'll update you at each stage.

Use these to reply quickly without stress.

Practice 2: Ask questions that guide buying
In every serious conversation, ask at least two guiding questions:

When do you need it?
What style do you prefer?
What is your budget range?
Do you want premium quality or the most affordable option?

Guiding questions reduce confusion and speed up decisions.

Practice 3: Feature customers weekly
Every week, post one customer-driven piece.

It can be:
A testimonial screenshot
A photo with a short story
A repeat customer appreciation

Always keep it respectful.
Always get permission.

Practice 4: Invite customers into the journey
This is the community part.

Invite customers to:
Vote between two designs
Suggest what they want next week
Ask questions in comments
Share a photo after using the product
Join a broadcast list for updates

When customers participate, they feel ownership.

Ownership creates loyalty.

8) Common mistakes that turn social media into noise
Let me name the traps clearly so you avoid them.

Posting without a purpose.
Chasing every trend.
Copying content that does not match your brand.
Ignoring messages and comments.
Overposting offers and discounts.
Using desperate language.
Arguing publicly with customers.
Changing platforms every week.
Measuring only likes instead of inquiries and sales.

If you avoid these, you are already ahead of many businesses.

9) How to measure progress (what matters, not vanity)
Here is what I track weekly:

Number of serious inquiries
Number of orders
Number of repeat customers
Number of referrals
Content posted (yes or no)
Engagement done (yes or no)

Vanity metrics like likes are not useless, but they are not the main signal.

The main signal is:
Are inquiries and sales increasing over time?

If yes, keep going.
If no, adjust your message, your offer clarity, or your engagement habits.

10) Final word: community is built by repeated respect
Social media mastery is not a secret trick.

It is repeated respect.

Respect in how you post.
Respect in how you reply.

Respect in how you deliver.
Respect in how you treat customers publicly.

When people feel respected, they return.
When people return, your business grows.
When your business grows, you gain freedom.

Build community, not noise.

In the next chapter, we will focus on mobile marketing, meaning how I use the phone-first reality of modern customers to drive sales through direct messaging, simple funnels, and fast follow-up that feels personal and professional.

Field Guides (Platform Playbooks)
User's Guide: How to Use Instagram to Build Your Brand

Instagram works best when you treat it like a storefront, not a scrapbook. When someone lands on your profile, they are asking one silent question: "Can I trust this business?" Your job is to answer that question fast with consistency, clarity, and proof.

1) Feed consistency: how I make my page look like one business

Consistency is not about being fancy. It is about being recognizable.

I keep four things consistent:

Visual rules

- Same light style (window light or shade)
- Same background style (clean, simple, controlled)
- Same angle style (repeat 2 to 3 angles)
- Same editing style (similar brightness and color temperature)

Content pillars (I pick 3 and repeat them)

- Proof (customer photos, testimonials, results)
- Process (behind-the-scenes, quality checks, packaging)
- Education (tips, mistakes to avoid, how to choose)

Post types (I rotate them like a menu)

- One "hero" product post
- One process post
- One customer story post
- One educational post

Series names (so people know what to expect)
I use repeatable series like:

- "Behind the Work"
- "Customer Story"
- "Quick Tip"
- "This Week's Slots"

When you repeat the same series names, your audience learns your rhythm. Rhythm builds familiarity. Familiarity builds trust.

2) Captions with emotion: how I sell without sounding desperate

Emotion in business captions is not drama. It is meaning. It is the feeling the customer wants when they buy.

Most customers want one of these feelings:

- Confidence
- Relief
- Pride
- Belonging
- Peace of mind

So I write captions that connect the product to a real feeling.

Here is my caption structure (simple, repeatable):

Line 1: Hook
A direct line that matches the customer's life.

Lines 2 to 5: The human point
What problem this solves, what you chose, what standard you kept.

Line 6: Proof
A short trust signal (timeline, finishing detail, customer feedback, repeat order, delivery discipline).

Last line: One clear next step
Message me, book, order, join list, pick option A or B.

Example (template you can copy):

- Hook: Workwear should make you feel ready, not restricted.
- Human point: I made this piece for long days and real movement, with clean finishing and a fit that respects comfort.
- Proof: Delivered in three days with one fitting.
- Next step: Message me your size and deadline and I'll guide you.

3) Community engagement: the habits that make Instagram pay you back

Posting is only half the job. The other half is relationships.

My daily engagement habit is simple:

15 minutes, twice a day

- Reply to comments
- Reply to DMs
- Leave 5 to 10 meaningful comments where my ideal customers already gather (local pages, niche pages, partner businesses)

My weekly habit:

- Feature one customer (photo, quote, or short story)
- Ask one good question (poll, "Which design?", "Which color?", "What do you struggle with?")
- Do one collaboration touch (feature swap, partner shout-out, joint offer)

4) Using account analytics to adjust what I post

I do not guess. I review performance weekly and make small changes.

Inside Instagram's professional account analytics, I pay attention to metrics like views, accounts reached, interactions, and accounts engaged, and I compare results across posts and reels over selectable timeframes. (Facebook)

My weekly review questions:

- Which post reached the most new people?
- Which post got the most saves or shares (strong buying signal)?
- Which post got the most profile visits or DMs?
- What format performed best (photo, carousel, reel)?
- What topic got the strongest response (proof, process, education)?

Then I make one change only:

- Post more of what got saves and shares
- Improve hooks on what got low reach
- Tighten captions if people watched but did not act
- Repeat winners with a new example

This is how the feed becomes a system instead of random posting.

My Instagram weekly plan (starter version)

- 3 posts per week: education, process, customer story
- stories most days: quick updates, polls, behind-the-scenes
- daily engagement: 30 minutes total
- weekly review: 20 minutes on Sunday

If you do this for 90 days, your page stops feeling like a hobby and starts feeling like a brand.

User's Guide: Building a WhatsApp Community for Your Business

WhatsApp is not a "social platform" in the usual sense. It is closer to a private room. That is why trust is everything. People do not want noise in WhatsApp. They want usefulness, clarity, and respect.

1) Choose the right structure: group, broadcast, or community

I choose based on how I want people to interact.

Group
Best for two-way conversation and community energy.

Broadcast list
Best for one-way updates (new stock, weekly slots, announcements) without chatter.

Community
Best when I need multiple groups under one roof (for example: announcements, support group, VIP buyers, resellers). WhatsApp Communities were built to organize multiple groups and improve admin control. (TechCrunch)

If I want order and growth at the same time, I use a community structure:

- One announcement channel for official updates
- Smaller groups for discussion by topic or customer type

WhatsApp has also added features for community-style groups like events and replies to announcements, designed to keep members organized while reducing clutter. (The Indian Express)

2) Starting a group the right way

Most business groups fail because they start with no rules and no welcome.

When I create a business group, I set these basics immediately:

Group name
Make it clear and specific (not cute, not vague).

Group description
One sentence about purpose.
One sentence about what to post.
One sentence about what not to post.

Admins
At least two admins if the group will grow.

Pinned message
The group rules and the ordering process live in the pinned message.

3) Welcoming members: my simple welcome flow
When a new member joins, I do not just say "welcome."

I use a short structure:

- Welcome line
- What this group is for
- How often I post
- How to order
- One rule about respect and spam
- One small question to invite participation

Example welcome message:
Welcome. This group is for updates, tips, and customer stories from my business. I post 3 times a week and I keep messages short. To order, message me directly with your deadline and what you want. Please do not drop unrelated links or forwards. Quick question: what are you here for, learning, ordering, or both?

This creates clarity and reduces chaos.

4) Posting content that keeps conversations alive
Conversation does not stay alive by accident. It stays alive because you lead it.

I use a weekly rhythm:

Monday
One short educational post (tip or mistake to avoid)

Wednesday
One behind-the-scenes update (photo or short clip)

Friday
One customer story or proof post (with permission)

Weekend
Optional: slots, pricing ranges, new arrivals

Then I use conversation prompts:

- "Which option fits you better, A or B?"
- "What is your biggest challenge with ordering online?"
- "What would you like me to share next week?"

I also use voice notes sometimes because they feel human and fast, but I keep them short.

5) Rules to protect trust (this is non-negotiable)
Trust dies fast in messaging spaces.

So I protect it with rules like:

- No spam, no unrelated links, no chain forwards
- No politics, no insults, no tribal fights
- No posting other people's phone numbers
- No private customer photos without permission
- Admins can remove repeated offenders

I enforce politely, but firmly.

If you do not protect the group, serious customers leave quietly, and only noise remains.

6) Turning the WhatsApp group into sales without being pushy
I do not sell daily.

I guide daily, and I offer weekly.

My soft selling method:

- teach, show process, share proof

- remind people how to order
- give clear slot windows (so urgency is real)

The result is simple: customers feel safe to buy because they have watched you behave consistently.

User's Guide: How to Use X to Boost Your Business

X is fast, public, and idea-driven. You do not win there by posting ads. You win by showing a brain, a voice, and a steady story.

I treat each post like one brick in a bigger wall. One post is small. A year of posts becomes a reputation.

1) Profile setup: my credibility checklist
Before posting, I make the profile clear:

- A clean profile photo (face or brand mark)
- One-line promise (what I help people do)
- One link (website, product page, or WhatsApp order link)
- A pinned post that explains: what I do, who it is for, how to work with me

If a stranger lands on your profile, they should understand you in 10 seconds.

2) Posting philosophy: purposeful, not random
My posting rule:
One post, one idea.

I rotate four post types:

- Education: tips, mistakes, explanations
- Proof: customer wins, results, feedback
- Process: behind-the-scenes thinking, standards, how I work
- Offer: clear services or products, with a simple next step

I keep offers limited. Too many offers makes people mute you.

3) Threads: how I turn knowledge into a brand story

Threads are one of the strongest tools on X because they let you teach in a connected sequence. X defines a thread as a series of connected posts from one person, created by composing a post and adding additional posts before publishing them together. (Help Center)

My thread template:

- Post 1: Hook (a strong claim or problem)
- Post 2: Why this matters (human consequence)
- Post 3 to 6: Steps or lessons (clear, practical)
- Post 7: Proof or example
- Final post: One next step (follow, message, order, read)

I keep threads tight. No long speeches. Just clean teaching.

4) Engagement: how I build presence without living on the app

X rewards conversation.

My engagement system:

- Reply to 10 relevant posts daily (short, useful replies)
- Quote post 2 times a week (add my view, not just repost)
- Thank people who share my work
- Avoid fights and sarcasm (they grow attention, not trust)

Consistency is what builds presence.

5) Simple weekly plan for X

- 5 short posts per week
- 2 threads per week
- daily replies (10 minutes morning, 10 minutes evening)
- 1 pinned "start here" post updated monthly

If you keep this for 6 months, you become familiar to the right people. Familiarity drives clicks, DMs, and referrals.

A User's Guide to LinkedIn for Business Growth

LinkedIn is where trust wears a suit. People buy there too, but they buy after credibility is established. You do not need to pretend to be big. You need to look reliable, specific, and consistent.

1) Setting up credibility: my profile as a sales asset

I build credibility through clarity.

Headline
Not a job title only. A promise.
Example: I help small businesses grow online using content, messaging, and simple systems.

About section
Short story plus proof:

- who I help
- what problems I solve
- what results I deliver
- how to work with me

Featured section
Put your best proof there:

- best case study post
- customer feedback
- portfolio link
- order link or booking link

Services
If relevant, list services with clear outcomes.

2) Networking with intention (not collecting random connections)

I do not connect with everyone.

I connect with:

- ideal customers

- partners who share the audience
- people in the same value space (referrals happen here)

My connection message is short:
Hello, I saw your work in _____. I help businesses with _____. Happy to connect.

Then I do not pitch immediately.

I build a relationship by:

- engaging with their posts
- sending a useful resource when it fits
- asking a real question

LinkedIn rewards professional behavior.

3) Content that works on LinkedIn
LinkedIn likes clarity and usefulness.

My best-performing post types are:

- mini case studies (problem, action, result)
- lessons learned from real work
- "how I do it" process posts
- customer proof posts (with permission)
- short educational posts

I avoid motivational noise. I write like a working professional.

4) Endorsements and recommendations: using social proof the right way
Two trust builders matter a lot on LinkedIn:

Skill endorsements
LinkedIn allows you to add skills (up to 100), and your 1st-degree connections can endorse those skills, strengthening your profile and helping discovery for related opportunities. (LinkedIn)

My approach:

- I add only skills I want to be known for
- I keep the top skills aligned with my offer
- I remove irrelevant skills that dilute my message

Recommendations
Recommendations are written commendations by LinkedIn members to recognize your work, and you can request them from 1st-degree connections you worked with. (LinkedIn)

My recommendation system:

- I ask right after a project win
- I make it easy by suggesting 3 bullet points they can mention
- I request one recommendation per strong project, not from everyone

Example ask (you can copy):
Hi _____. Thanks again for working with me on _____. If you're comfortable, could you write a short LinkedIn recommendation about our work? If helpful, you can mention: what problem we solved, what you liked about my communication, and the result. I appreciate it.

That message is respectful and clear.

5) Simple weekly LinkedIn growth plan

- Post 2 to 3 times per week
- Comment thoughtfully on 15 posts per week (not "nice post" comments)
- Send 5 connection requests per week to ideal people
- Request one recommendation per month (from the strongest work)

LinkedIn growth is slow, but it is durable. The leads tend to be higher quality because trust is built in public.

Closing note I use across all platforms

The platform is not the business. The platform is a road. Your business is the destination.

So I build on any platform using the same standards:

- clarity of offer
- proof of quality
- respect in communication
- consistency over time

Chapter Eight: The Power of Mobile Marketing

If you want to understand how customers really buy today, forget the laptop-first fantasy. Most people do not "browse the internet" the way marketers describe it. They live on a phone. They see your work on a small screen. They make decisions while walking, commuting, eating, or lying in bed at night. They message you with one hand. They lose signal. They switch from Wi-Fi to mobile data. Their battery drops. Their cash is often in a mobile wallet, not a bank card.

That reality is not a problem. It is an advantage, if you build for it.

Mobile marketing is not a trend. It is simply meeting customers where they already live. And in many places, especially where connectivity is unstable, mobile marketing becomes the most practical and reliable way to sell.

In this chapter, I will show you how I reach customers on mobile using tools like WhatsApp, mobile-friendly pages, and mobile payments. Then I will help you build a mobile-first communication flow that carries a customer from inquiry to payment to delivery to repeat purchase. Finally, you will set up WhatsApp Business tools, create a quick product catalog, and build a weekly message plan you can sustain.

Why mobile wins in real business

I have learned one rule through experience.

When connectivity is unstable, the business that stays simple wins.

Mobile buyers want:

Speed
Clarity
Short steps
Low data usage
Fast replies
Predictable updates
Proof that you are real

When you design your marketing and sales process around those needs, customers feel safe. Safety is the real reason people buy.

A customer does not pay because your caption is clever. A customer pays because they feel:

I understand what I'm buying.
I trust this seller.
I know what happens next.
If something goes wrong, this seller will respond.

Mobile marketing is the discipline of building that feeling through a phone-first path.

The mobile-first mindset: I build a path, not a pile of tools

Many business owners collect tools like trophies.

They have:

A page here
A profile there
A link tree
A catalog somewhere
A payment option that works only sometimes
A delivery rider with no clear process
A customer list with no routine

Then they wonder why they feel overwhelmed.

I do it differently. I build a path.

A path has five connected parts:

Discovery (how customers find me)
Contact (how customers reach me)
Clarity (how customers understand the offer and price)
Confirmation (how customers pay and lock the order)
Completion (how I deliver and follow up)

Mobile marketing is about tightening those parts until nothing feels confusing.

The mobile tools I rely on (and why)

I keep my tool stack simple. In most small businesses, the best mobile stack looks like this:

WhatsApp Business as the main communication channel
A lightweight "home page" (website or store page) that loads fast on mobile
Mobile payment options that match how customers actually pay
A simple delivery update routine that reduces anxiety
A customer broadcast routine that keeps the relationship alive

Let's break each one down in a way you can apply immediately.

WhatsApp as the sales engine

WhatsApp is powerful because it feels personal and fast. People trust messages more than ads. In many regions, WhatsApp is where business happens, even when other platforms fail.

But WhatsApp becomes chaos if you run it like a normal chat app. The goal is to run it like a business system.

Set up WhatsApp Business the right way

If you use WhatsApp Business, treat the setup like a storefront sign.

Your Business Profile should include:

Business name (consistent across platforms)
Short description (what you sell, who it's for, what promise you keep)
Location or service area (even if you deliver)
Hours (so customers know when to expect replies)
Email or backup contact (optional but helpful)

The goal is simple: when a stranger messages you, they should instantly feel you are real.

Use these WhatsApp Business tools to save time and increase trust

Here are the tools I recommend and how I use them.

Greeting message
This is your automatic first handshake. It reduces customer anxiety.

Example greeting:
Thanks for reaching out. Tell me what you want, your deadline, and your budget range, and I'll guide you with options.

Away message
This protects you when you sleep or travel. It also prevents customers from feeling ignored.

Example away message:
Thanks for your message. I'm currently away. I will reply within 12 hours. If your request is urgent, please include your deadline.

Quick replies
Quick replies turn your best answers into saved templates. This is where you win on mobile. You do not want to type the same explanation 50 times.

Create quick replies for:
Pricing ranges
Order steps
Payment options
Delivery areas and fees
Fitting or booking instructions
Refund or adjustment policy
Proof links (portfolio, customer stories, catalog)

Labels
Labels help you organize customers so you stop losing leads.

Labels I use:
New inquiry
Needs pricing

Waiting for payment
Order confirmed
In production
Out for delivery
Delivered
Follow up needed
Repeat customer
VIP

Catalog
The catalog is your mobile showroom. It reduces back-and-forth questions and moves people faster to decision.

Even if you sell services, you can still use a catalog by listing service packages.

The biggest rule: keep WhatsApp low-friction
A mobile buyer will not tolerate long steps.

If ordering takes too long, they abandon.

Your WhatsApp flow should aim for:

Short questions
Fast clarity
Simple choices
Clear next step

Instead of asking 10 questions, ask 3 strong questions that qualify and guide:

What do you want?
When do you need it?
What is your budget range?

Those three questions filter out noise and attract serious buyers.

Mobile-friendly pages that load fast and sell clearly
Some business owners depend only on WhatsApp. That can work, but you still need a "home base" page for three reasons:

It gives proof at a glance
It answers common questions without long chats
It works even when you are busy and cannot reply instantly

Your mobile page can be a full website, but it does not need to be. It can be one simple page that does one job: help customers understand and act.

What a mobile-friendly page must include
On mobile, attention is short. Your page must be simple.

Your page should have:

A clear offer statement
A short list of best products or services
Proof (photos, testimonials, examples)
Pricing guidance (ranges, not confusion)
How to order (simple steps)
Contact button (WhatsApp link)
Payment options (brief)
Delivery info (brief)
Policies (short and clear)

If your page loads slowly or is cluttered, it fails.

How I keep mobile pages fast, especially with weak internet
I use these practical rules:

Keep images light
Use fewer images, but higher quality
Avoid heavy sliders and animations
Avoid auto-playing videos on the page
Use short paragraphs and clear spacing

Put the order button near the top
Use one primary call to action

If you are not technical, you can still achieve this by choosing a simple website theme and resisting the urge to add many extras.

Remember: speed is a sales skill.

Mobile payments: remove friction, increase confidence
Payment is where many mobile sales fail.

Not because customers do not want to pay, but because the process feels uncertain.

A customer asks:
How do I pay?
Will I get confirmation?
What if the seller disappears?
What if delivery delays?

Your job is to make payment feel safe and predictable.

Payment options that work well on mobile
The best payment options depend on your region, but the principle is universal:

Use what customers already use.

Common mobile-first payment options:
Mobile money (fastest for many markets)
Bank transfer (for higher trust buyers)
Card payments (if you have a reliable link)
Cash on delivery (only if safe and controlled)
Deposit plus balance on delivery (often the best compromise)

The most important payment practice: confirm and document
After payment, customers need reassurance fast.

I always send:
A short confirmation message
A receipt reference (even if simple)
A timeline and next update point

Example:
Payment received, thank you. Your order is confirmed. Next update in 24 hours when I begin production. Delivery on Friday by 4 pm.

That one message reduces anxiety and prevents unnecessary follow-up spam.

Mobile marketing in unstable connectivity: how I stay reliable when the network is not

In places with unstable connectivity, customers do not expect perfection, but they expect effort and communication.

So I build redundancy.

Redundancy means I plan for failure

If WhatsApp fails, what happens?
If mobile data drops, what happens?
If a customer's phone is off, what happens?
If delivery delays, what happens?

A mobile-first business must have backup habits.

Here are mine:

Use text-first communication
Images are powerful, but text carries the deal when data is low.

Send compressed photos when needed
One clear photo is better than ten heavy ones.

Use voice notes carefully
Voice notes can be human and fast, but keep them short. Many people cannot listen at work.

Keep a simple "order summary" message
So if the chat scrolls, you can resend the summary.

Have a backup contact method
A phone call option or SMS for urgent delivery coordination.

Set expectations about response times
So customers do not assume you vanished.

Reliability is not about perfect internet. It is about predictable behavior.

What you build: a mobile-first communication flow
Now we build the flow you will use every day.

This is your phone-first sales pipeline.

It has six stages:

Inquiry
Qualification
Pricing and options
Order confirmation
Delivery updates
Aftercare and retention

You can run this flow entirely on WhatsApp, supported by your mobile page and payment method.

Stage 1: Inquiry
Goal: respond fast and guide.

Reply template:
Thanks for reaching out. What do you want, when do you need it, and what is your budget range?

Why this works:
It is short, professional, and it filters serious buyers.

Stage 2: Qualification
Goal: confirm fit and prevent wrong orders.

Ask the minimum questions needed to deliver well.

For products:
Size, quantity, color or variation, delivery location

For services:
Scope, deadline, budget range, any examples they like

Then summarize:
So you want _____ by _____ with a budget range of _____. Correct?

This summary prevents misunderstanding.

Stage 3: Pricing and options
Goal: present choices, not confusion.

Give 2 to 3 options only.

Example structure:
Option A: basic, price, timeline
Option B: standard, price, timeline
Option C: premium, price, timeline

Then ask:
Which option do you want?

Too many options creates delay.

Pricing rule:
Be clear about what affects price. Customers tolerate price better when they understand it.

Stage 4: Order confirmation
Goal: lock the order with payment and clear steps.

Confirmation message template:
Great. To confirm your order, send payment to _____. After payment, please share the confirmation screenshot or reference. Once confirmed, I will begin and update you at _____.

If you use deposit:
To confirm your slot, deposit _____ today, and pay the balance on delivery.

Then, once paid:
Payment received. Order confirmed. Delivery date and time: _____.
Next update: _____.

Stage 5: Delivery updates
Goal: reduce anxiety and build trust.

Most customers do not need daily updates. They need predictable updates.

I use a simple rule:
Update at meaningful milestones.

Milestones:
Order confirmed
Work started
Mid-progress check (optional)
Packaging
Out for delivery
Delivered

Your updates should be short:

Work started. Everything on schedule.
Packaging now. Delivery today between 2 and 4 pm.
Out for delivery. Rider contact: _____.

This reduces "Are you there?" messages and makes you look professional.

Stage 6: Aftercare and retention
Goal: turn one sale into a relationship.

After delivery message:
Thanks again. How is everything so far? If you need any adjustment or support, tell me.

Then ask for proof:
If you are happy with it, can you share a photo or a short feedback line? It helps people trust my work.

Then retention:
I share updates every Friday. If you want, I can add you to my weekly broadcast list.

That is how one customer becomes part of your community.

What you build: a simple customer broadcast routine
Broadcast is how you stay visible without begging. It is how you remind customers that you exist, that you are active, and that you have standards.

But broadcast fails when it becomes spam.

So I keep it predictable, useful, and short.

My broadcast rules
I do not broadcast daily.
I do not forward unrelated content.
I do not use long paragraphs.
I do not push discounts every time.

I broadcast:
Help, proof, availability

That balance keeps trust.

The weekly broadcast structure I recommend
One message per week is enough to start.

A simple weekly message can include:

A short tip (education)
A short proof (customer story or result)
An availability note (slots, new stock, booking window)
A clear next step (reply with X to order)

Example weekly broadcast message:
Quick tip: if you want a shirt that stays sharp, choose fabric that holds shape, and always confirm fitting. This week's highlight: delivered 3 office shirts with clean finishing and on-time delivery. Slots available for next week: Monday to Thursday. Reply "ORDER" with your deadline and I'll guide you.

Short. Useful. Professional.

Segmenting your broadcast (optional, but powerful)
As you grow, segment customers:

VIP customers
New leads
Past customers
Service type A customers
Service type B customers

This allows you to send relevant updates instead of blasting everyone.

Relevance is respect.

Practice: set up WhatsApp Business tools, create a quick product catalog, build a weekly message plan
Now we do the practical work.

Practice step 1: Set up WhatsApp Business tools
Set up:
Business profile (description, hours, location)
Greeting message

Away message
Quick replies
Labels

Quick reply templates to create today:

Inquiry template
Pricing template
Order confirmation template
Payment received template
Delivery update template
After delivery follow-up template
Testimonial request template
Broadcast invite template

If you do this, you will immediately save time and respond faster.

Practice step 2: Create a quick product catalog

Catalog setup rules:

Use clear product names
Use one strong photo per item
Add short descriptions that focus on benefit
Include pricing ranges or starting prices
Add "how to order" note in descriptions if useful

If you sell services, list packages like:

Basic package
Standard package
Premium package

Each with:
What's included
Timeline
Price range

The catalog should reduce questions, not create more.

Practice step 3: Build a weekly message plan

Your weekly plan should include:

One behind-the-scenes update
One customer story or proof
One educational tip
One availability or offer message (optional)
One broadcast message (weekly)

If you want a simple schedule:

Monday: educational post (tip)
Wednesday: behind-the-scenes (process photo)
Friday: customer story (proof)
Saturday: weekly broadcast (short and useful)

The goal is not volume. The goal is rhythm.

The mobile-first advantage: why this chapter matters

When you build mobile-first, you become easier to buy from.

Your competition may have good products, but many sellers lose customers through friction:

Slow replies
Confusing pricing
No clear ordering steps
No updates
Payment uncertainty
Delivery stress
No follow-up

Mobile-first marketing solves those issues by making your business behave like a professional system.

And the best part is this:

You do not need perfect internet.
You do not need expensive tools.
You need clear steps and consistent habits.

If you do the work in this chapter, customers will start describing your business with the words every entrepreneur wants to hear:

Reliable.
Clear.
Professional.
Easy to buy from.

Next, we move into how to convert this attention and engagement into consistent sales using simple funnels, customer relationship habits, and offer design that fits mobile buying behavior.

Chapter Nine: Building Customer Relationships

Most small businesses do not fail because they cannot get customers once. They fail because customers do not return.

A first sale can happen by luck. A repeat sale happens because you earned trust.

If your growth depends only on finding new customers every week, you will feel exhausted. You will spend money and time chasing attention. You will ride emotional waves: one good week, one dead week, one stressful week, then panic.

That is not stable business.

Stable business is built on relationships.

Relationships are what turn one sale into five sales, one customer into a referral source, and one busy season into a long-term reputation.

This chapter is about how I keep customers after the first sale through service, follow-up, community, feedback loops, and loyalty habits, so growth is not a one-time spike.

And I will make it practical. You will build a customer journey plan and simple scripts for replies, updates, and problem-solving. Then you will create a follow-up message sequence, invite reviews, and turn feedback into real improvements.

1) The real meaning of customer relationships

Customer relationships are not about being "nice."

They are about being reliable.

A strong customer relationship means a customer believes:

This seller will respond.
This seller will deliver.
This seller will correct issues.

This seller respects me.
This seller is consistent.

That belief is worth more than any advertisement.

In business, trust is the cheapest marketing and the most expensive thing to lose.

So when I talk about customer relationships, I mean systems and habits that protect trust.

2) The relationship economy: why repeat customers matter

Repeat customers do three powerful things:

They lower your marketing cost.
You do not have to convince them again.

They raise your profit.
The second sale is easier, faster, and cheaper.

They create referrals.
Happy customers talk, and people trust friends more than ads.

That is why I focus on retention, not only acquisition.

Acquisition brings customers in.
Retention keeps money circulating in your business.

If you want growth without burnout, retention must be a priority.

3) What I teach: how I keep customers after the first sale

I use five levers to keep customers:

Service that feels professional
Follow-up that feels human
Community that feels safe
Feedback loops that improve the business
Loyalty habits that reward repeat behavior

Let's break them down.

A) Service that feels professional

Most relationship problems are actually service problems.

A customer complains not only because the product is wrong, but because they feel ignored, disrespected, or uncertain.

Professional service has four signals:

Clarity
Speed
Updates
Respect

Clarity means:
The customer knows what they are buying, how to order, how payment works, and what delivery looks like.

Speed means:
The customer feels you are present and responsive.

Updates means:
The customer does not have to chase you. You communicate milestones.

Respect means:
Your tone stays calm and professional, even when the customer is difficult.

If you do these four consistently, relationships become easier.

B) Follow-up that feels human

Follow-up is where many businesses lose repeat sales.

They deliver, then disappear.

The customer feels:
They got what they needed, but there is no relationship.

So I follow up after delivery.

Not with desperation. With care and structure.

Follow-up does three jobs:

Confirms satisfaction
Invites feedback
Opens the door for the next purchase

A customer who feels cared for returns more often.

C) Community that feels safe

Community is a relationship amplifier.

It keeps customers connected to your brand even when they are not buying.

If you build a WhatsApp broadcast list, a customer group, or even an Instagram community, you are building a space where your brand stays present.

But community must feel safe.

If your group becomes spam and noise, serious customers leave.

So the community needs:
Rules
Consistency
Useful content
Respectful tone

D) Feedback loops that improve the business

Every business has friction.

The difference between a weak business and a strong one is how it responds to friction.

Weak business:
Ignores feedback or gets defensive.

Strong business:
Collects feedback, identifies patterns, and improves.

Feedback is not an attack. It is data.

If you use it well, your quality rises and your complaints reduce.

E) Loyalty habits that reward repeat behavior
Loyalty is not always a "points system."

Loyalty can be simple:

Priority slots for repeat customers
Small thank-you bonuses
Free delivery after a certain number of orders
VIP broadcast list
Early access to new stock
Personal follow-up and care

The purpose is not to give away profit. The purpose is to create belonging.

People return where they feel valued.

4) What you build: a customer journey plan
Now we build the practical tool.

A customer journey plan is the map of how you treat customers at each stage:

Before purchase
During purchase
After purchase

This plan prevents you from improvising.

When you improvise, service quality becomes inconsistent. Inconsistency kills trust.

Customer Journey Plan (copy and fill)

Stage 1: Before purchase (discovery to inquiry)
Customer needs:
Clarity, proof, fast response

My actions:
Clear offer statement
Visible proof (photos, testimonials)
Clear order steps
Fast inquiry reply
Guiding questions to qualify customer

My scripts:
Inquiry reply script
Pricing script
Order steps script

Stage 2: During purchase (ordering to delivery)
Customer needs:
Confirmation, updates, predictable timeline

My actions:
Order summary confirmation
Payment confirmation message
Milestone updates
Delivery coordination
Respectful communication

My scripts:
Payment received script
Work started update
Packaging update
Out for delivery update

Stage 3: After purchase (delivery to repeat)
Customer needs:
Care, problem resolution, invitation to return

My actions:
Satisfaction check message
Feedback request
Review request (public)
Testimonial request (private)
Broadcast invite
Loyalty offer (if applicable)

My scripts:
After delivery check-in
Problem-solving script
Review request script
Repeat order invitation script

That is the journey plan.

Now we fill it with scripts.

5) What you build: simple scripts for replies, updates, and problem-solving

Scripts are not robotic. Scripts protect your energy and protect customer experience.

When you are busy, scripts help you stay consistent.

I will give you a full set of scripts you can copy and adjust.

A) Before purchase scripts

Inquiry reply script:
Thanks for reaching out. What do you want, when do you need it, and what is your budget range? I'll guide you with options.

Pricing script:
Pricing depends on the design and size. For your request, the range is ____ to ____. If you share your preferred style and deadline, I'll confirm the exact price and timeline.

Order steps script:
To order: 1) confirm your option and deadline, 2) make payment

(or deposit) to lock the slot, 3) I send confirmation and timeline, 4) I update you at key stages, 5) delivery or pickup.

Proof script:
Here are a few examples of recent work. If you tell me what style you like, I can recommend the closest option.

B) During purchase scripts

Order summary script:
Just confirming: you ordered _____ (quantity, style, color/size) for delivery/pickup on _____ at _____. Total price: _____. Payment method: _____. Correct?

Payment received script:
Payment received, thank you. Your order is confirmed. I will start on _____ and send the next update by _____.

Work started update:
Work has started and everything is on schedule. Next update will be _____.

Packaging update:
Your order is packaged and ready. Delivery today between _____ and _____. If anything changes, I will update you.

Out for delivery update:
Out for delivery now. Rider contact: _____. Please keep your phone available. Thank you.

Delivered confirmation:
Delivered successfully. Thank you for trusting me. I appreciate it.

C) After purchase scripts

Satisfaction check message:
How is everything so far? If you need any adjustment or support, tell me and I'll help.

Feedback request:
If you have one minute, what did you like most about the experience, and what can I improve?

Testimonial request:
If you're happy with it, can you share a short feedback line I can post (or a photo if you're comfortable)? It helps people trust my work.

Review request (public platform):
If you don't mind, please leave a quick review here. It helps my small business grow and helps other customers feel safe to order.

Repeat invitation:
Whenever you need another ____ (product/service), message me early and I'll prioritize your slot. Thank you again.

Broadcast invite:
I share useful tips and weekly updates once a week. If you want, I can add you to my broadcast list.

D) Problem-solving scripts (the relationship saver)

Problems happen. The relationship is defined by how you handle them.

Here is my problem-solving structure:

Acknowledge
Clarify
Offer options
Confirm solution
Follow through

Acknowledgement script:
Thanks for telling me. I understand the concern, and I want to fix it.

Clarify script:
Can you share a photo or explain exactly what feels wrong? I want to understand clearly.

Options script:
Here are the options: 1) adjustment/replacement by ____, 2) partial refund if adjustment is not possible, 3) alternative solution ____. Which one works best for you?

Confirm script:
Understood. We will do ____. Timeline: ____. I will update you at ____. Thank you for your patience.

Follow-through script:
Update: I have completed ____. Here is the next step ____. Thank you again.

This structure turns conflict into trust-building.

Many customers become loyal after a well-handled problem.

6) Practice: create a follow-up message sequence

Now you will create a follow-up sequence.

This sequence is not spam. It is customer care.

The simplest sequence has four messages.

Follow-up sequence (copy and use)

Message 1 (same day delivery):
Delivered. Thank you for trusting me. If anything needs adjustment or support, tell me.

Message 2 (1 to 2 days later):
How is it going so far? I want to confirm everything feels right.

Message 3 (3 to 5 days later):
If you have one minute, what did you like most, and what should I improve?

Message 4 (7 to 10 days later):
If you're happy with the result, can you share a short review or feedback? It helps other customers trust my work. Also, I post

weekly updates once a week, want me to add you to my broadcast list?

That is enough.

Notice what I did:
Care first
Feedback second
Review third
Retention fourth

Most businesses do it backwards.

They ask for reviews before they confirm satisfaction. That feels selfish.

7) Practice: invite reviews the right way
Reviews are social proof. They reduce doubt for future buyers.

But asking wrongly can feel pushy.

So I use three rules:

Ask only after a good experience.
Make it easy.
Be respectful, not needy.

Review request message (copy)
If you're happy with your order, could you leave a quick review? Even one sentence helps other customers feel safe to order. I really appreciate it.

If you want, add a direct link or simple instructions.

If you are using WhatsApp, you can still collect private reviews and share them as testimonials (with permission).

8) Practice: turn feedback into product and service improvements

This is where the business matures.

Feedback is only useful if it changes something.

So I run a simple feedback loop.

Step 1: Collect feedback weekly

Every week, note:

What customers praised
What customers complained about
What customers requested

Even 10 notes are enough.

Step 2: Identify patterns

Do not react to one angry person.
React to repeating patterns.

Examples of patterns:
Customers always ask about timelines
Customers always get confused about pricing
Customers love your finishing but hate slow replies
Customers want more options
Customers complain about packaging

Patterns show where improvement matters most.

Step 3: Choose one improvement per week

Do not overwhelm yourself.

One improvement per week is enough:

Rewrite your pricing message.
Improve packaging.
Add delivery updates.

Create a catalog.
Adjust photo quality.
Change how you confirm orders.

Small weekly improvements compound into a strong business.

Step 4: Communicate improvements
When you improve, tell customers.

Example:
Based on customer feedback, I now send delivery updates at each stage so you feel confident and informed.

This tells customers:
I listen.
I improve.
I respect them.

That strengthens relationships.

9) Loyalty habits that keep customers close
Now let's talk loyalty without complicated systems.

You can build loyalty with simple habits.

Loyalty habit ideas (choose two)
Priority booking:
Repeat customers get first access to slots.

Small surprise bonus:
A small add-on or discount after the third purchase.

VIP list:
VIP customers receive early updates and availability.

Thank-you message:
A personal thank-you note after delivery.

Anniversary follow-up:
After 30 days, check in: how is it holding up?

Referral reward:
If a customer refers someone who buys, offer a small reward.

The key is to keep loyalty rewards sustainable.

Do not destroy profit. Build belonging.

10) The relationship dashboard: what I track

If you do not track relationships, you will guess.

Here is what I track weekly:

Number of new customers
Number of repeat customers
Number of referrals
Number of complaints
Number of reviews collected
Average response time
On-time delivery rate

These numbers tell you if your relationships are strong.

Growth without retention is fragile.

Retention with service discipline is durable.

11) The final lesson: relationships are a system, not a mood

Some days you will feel tired.

If relationships depend on your mood, customers will feel inconsistency.

So I build relationships through scripts, routines, and predictable behavior.

Predictability creates trust.
Trust creates loyalty.
Loyalty creates stability.

This is how you grow without depending on one-time spikes.

In the next chapter, we will move deeper into conversion and selling systems, where we turn attention, engagement, and relationships into steady revenue through clear offers, simple funnels, and repeatable sales habits.

PART FOUR: MEASURING SUCCESS AND GROWTH

Chapter Ten: Tracking Your Results

If I do not measure my business, I am not really running a business. I am running a mood.

One week feels busy, so I assume I am growing.
One week feels quiet, so I assume I am failing.
One post gets likes, so I assume I found the secret.
One week has no sales, so I panic and change everything.

That cycle is expensive. It wastes time, energy, and confidence.

Tracking results is the discipline that saves me from guessing. It helps me see what is working, what is not, and what to adjust next. It also keeps me calm, because I stop treating every day like a verdict on my future.

In this chapter, I teach how I measure what matters using simple analytics so I stop guessing and start improving with evidence. You will build a one-page scorecard that tracks traffic, engagement, inquiries, conversions, and repeat customers. Then you will build a weekly review habit that links results back to actions, so you know exactly what to repeat, what to fix, and what to stop doing.

This is not about complicated dashboards. This is about a small business system that gives you clarity every week.

1) Why most entrepreneurs stay stuck: they do work, but they don't learn

Many small businesses do a lot of activity:

They post.
They reply.
They deliver.
They run promotions.
They try new platforms.
They change prices.
They redesign their pages.

But they do not know which action caused which result.

So they keep doing random work and hoping for a breakthrough.

I do the opposite. I use tracking to learn.

Tracking helps me answer questions like:

Which platform is sending me the most serious inquiries?
Which posts lead to WhatsApp messages, not only likes?
Which week had the highest conversion rate, and what did I do differently?
Are repeat customers increasing or decreasing?
Am I growing because of new customers, or because my service is improving and people return?

These questions turn business into a process, not a gamble.

2) The truth about "analytics": it is simply counting what matters

Analytics sounds technical, but for small business, it is simple:

Count what matters.
Review weekly.
Make one or two changes.
Repeat.

If you can count, you can do analytics.

The danger is not that analytics is hard.
The danger is measuring the wrong things.

If you measure only vanity numbers, you will feel good and still be broke.

Vanity numbers include:
Likes without inquiries
Followers without sales
Views without conversions

Those numbers can be useful, but they are not the score.

The score is what leads to money and stability:
Inquiries, conversions, repeat customers, referrals, and reliable delivery.

3) The five stages I track in every business
Every business, whether it is tailoring, baking, digital services, or local retail, follows the same flow:

1. People see you (traffic)
2. People react (engagement)
3. People reach out (inquiries)
4. People buy (conversions)
5. People return (repeat customers)

If I track those five stages, I can diagnose where the problem is.

Example diagnosis:

High traffic + low inquiries:
My message is unclear, my proof is weak, or my call to action is missing.

High inquiries + low conversions:
My pricing explanation is weak, my process is confusing, my response time is slow, or trust breaks before payment.

High conversions + low repeat customers:
My product is not consistent, delivery is unreliable, aftercare is missing, or I am not building loyalty.

Tracking turns "I don't know why" into "I know what to fix."

4) What you build: the one-page scorecard
Your scorecard is a single page you can update weekly in 10 to 20 minutes.

You can keep it in:
A notebook
A phone note
A simple spreadsheet
A printed sheet

The tool does not matter.
Consistency matters.

Here is the scorecard structure I use.

The One-Page Scorecard (Weekly)
Below is the exact layout. Copy it as-is and fill it weekly.

A) Traffic (who saw you)

- Profile visits (Instagram, Facebook, TikTok, LinkedIn, X)
- Website visits (if you have a site)
- Reach (accounts reached)
- Views (reels/video views, story views)

B) Engagement (who reacted and cared)

- Saves (strong buying signal)
- Shares (strong buying signal)
- Comments
- DMs started from posts
- Link clicks (if you use links)

C) Inquiries (who raised their hand)

- WhatsApp chats started (new inquiries)
- DMs that asked about price or ordering
- Calls (if you take calls)
- Walk-ins (if you have a physical shop)

D) Conversions (who paid)

- Number of orders

- Conversion rate (orders ÷ inquiries)
- Revenue (total)
- Average order value (revenue ÷ orders)

E) Repeat customers (who returned)

- Number of repeat customers this week
- Repeat rate (repeat customers ÷ total customers)
- Referrals (new customers who came through someone)

You can add a small "service quality" line if you want to protect your reputation:

- On-time delivery rate (delivered on time ÷ total orders)
- Complaints (count)
- Refunds/returns (count)

Keep it one page. Do not overbuild.

5) Definitions that keep your tracking clean

If you do not define metrics, you will track inconsistently. So I define them clearly.

Here are the definitions I use:

Traffic:
The number of people who had a chance to notice me.

Engagement:
The number of people who reacted in a way that shows interest.

Inquiry:
A message or call where someone asks about buying, pricing, ordering, availability, or booking.

Conversion:
A confirmed paid order (or a confirmed deposit if you use deposits).

Repeat customer:
A customer who bought before and bought again.

Referral:
A new customer who came because another customer recommended me.

Conversion rate:
Orders ÷ inquiries (weekly)

Repeat rate:
Repeat customers ÷ total customers (weekly)

Average order value:
Revenue ÷ number of orders

These definitions prevent confusion.

6) Where I get the numbers (simple sources)

You do not need fancy tools. Most numbers are already on your phone.

Traffic and engagement sources

- Instagram Professional Dashboard
- Facebook Page Insights
- TikTok analytics (if you use it)
- LinkedIn analytics
- X analytics (if available to you)
- Website stats (basic platform stats, or a simple analytics plugin)

Inquiry sources

- WhatsApp Business "labels" (count new inquiries)
- DMs (count serious buying messages)
- Call log (if calls are part of your process)
- Simple walk-in tally (if you run a physical shop)

Conversion sources

- Payment confirmations
- Order log (even a notebook log)
- Mobile money records, bank transfer history, receipts

Repeat and referral sources

- Customer list (tag repeat customers)
- WhatsApp labels ("repeat customer," "VIP")
- A simple question in your inquiry script:
  How did you hear about me?

That one question helps you track referrals and winning channels.

7) The key idea: leading metrics vs lagging metrics

To improve faster, I separate metrics into two types:

Leading metrics:
Actions and early signals I can influence this week.

Lagging metrics:
Results that show up after leading metrics do their job.

Examples:

Leading:
Number of posts published
Number of DMs replied within 1 hour
Number of comments I left on other pages
Number of stories posted
Number of follow-up messages sent
Number of testimonials collected

Lagging:
Revenue
Orders
Repeat customers

If I focus only on lagging metrics, I feel powerless.
If I track leading metrics, I see what I can control.

This is how I stay disciplined even when sales are slow.

8) Linking results back to actions (the part that makes tracking powerful)

Tracking becomes valuable only when it tells me what action caused the result.

So every week, I record actions next to numbers.

I do not only write:
Reach: 18,000
Inquiries: 22
Orders: 8

I also write:
This week I posted 3 customer stories.
I posted 2 behind-the-scenes reels.
I replied within 30 minutes on weekdays.
I followed up with 10 warm leads.
I ran a small collaboration feature.

Now I can see cause and effect.

The simplest "action log" I use
Under the scorecard, I write:

Actions I did this week:

- Posts: ___
- Stories: ___
- Reels/videos: ___
- Customer features: ___
- Collaborations: ___
- Follow-ups sent: ___
- Broadcast sent: yes/no
- Response time goal met: yes/no

Now I can compare week to week.

9) How I use tracking to diagnose business problems
Here are common patterns and what they usually mean.

Pattern 1: Traffic high, engagement low
Meaning:
People see your content, but it does not connect.

Fix:

- Improve your first line (hook)
- Improve photo quality and clarity
- Post more proof and process
- Make your captions simpler and more direct
- Use one clear call to action

Pattern 2: Engagement high, inquiries low
Meaning:
People like the content, but they do not know what to do next or do not feel safe enough to buy.

Fix:

- Add clear "how to order" steps
- Add pricing ranges
- Add more proof (testimonials, customer photos)
- Add "message me" invitations in posts and stories
- Use stronger questions to pull people into conversation

Pattern 3: Inquiries high, conversions low
Meaning:
People are interested, but you are losing them in the sales chat.

Fix:

- Improve response speed
- Use a clear pricing menu (2 to 3 options)
- Summarize the order clearly

- Build trust with milestone updates
- Reduce friction in payment and delivery steps

Pattern 4: Conversions good, repeat customers low
Meaning:
Your first sale works, but you are not building retention.

Fix:

- Add follow-up sequence
- Invite reviews and testimonials
- Build a broadcast routine
- Offer priority slots or a small loyalty reward
- Improve consistency in delivery and quality

Pattern 5: Repeat customers rising, traffic stable
Meaning:
You are building a strong base. This is excellent.

Fix:

- Keep retention strong
- Add one growth lever: collaboration, referrals, or one new platform
- Do not abandon what is already working

Tracking tells you which pattern you are living in.

10) What you build: the weekly review habit

The weekly review is where growth happens.

If I skip reviews, I repeat mistakes.
If I review weekly, I improve weekly.

This review does not need hours. It needs honesty.

My weekly review routine (30 to 45 minutes)
Step 1: Collect the numbers (10–15 minutes)
Fill the scorecard.

Do not overthink. Just record.

Step 2: Record the actions (5 minutes)
Write what you actually did this week.

Not what you planned. What you did.

Step 3: Answer five review questions (10–15 minutes)

1. What improved this week?
2. What dropped this week?
3. What action likely caused the improvement?
4. What action likely caused the drop?
5. What is the one change I will test next week?

Step 4: Choose one weekly experiment (5 minutes)
This is critical.

Do not change ten things at once.
Change one thing so you can see the effect.

Examples of weekly experiments:

- Post 2 customer stories instead of 1
- Add pricing ranges to every caption
- Reply within 30 minutes for 5 days
- Send one broadcast message every Friday
- Add one collaboration feature
- Add one behind-the-scenes reel per week
- Add an order summary message to every inquiry

One change. One week. Then measure.

Step 5: Plan next week's minimums (5 minutes)
I set small minimum targets that I can keep even during stress.

Example minimums:

- 3 posts

- 5 stories
- 20 minutes daily engagement
- Follow up with 10 warm leads
- 1 customer feature

Minimums create consistency.

Consistency creates growth.

11) The scorecard in action: a sample week

Here is a simple example to show how this works.

Week 1
Traffic:

- Reach: 12,400
- Profile visits: 420

Engagement:

- Saves: 38
- Shares: 19
- Comments: 26
- DMs started: 14

Inquiries:

- WhatsApp inquiries: 18

Conversions:

- Orders: 6
- Conversion rate: 6 ÷ 18 = 33%
- Revenue: 240,000
- Average order value: 40,000

Repeat:

- Repeat customers: 2

- Referrals: 1

Actions:

- Posted 3 times (1 process, 1 education, 1 customer story)
- Replied within 1 hour most days
- Sent 1 broadcast

Weekly learning:
Customer story post drove most DMs.
Broadcast drove one repeat order.

Weekly experiment:
Next week I will publish 2 customer stories and 1 process post (instead of only 1 customer story).

Week 2
Traffic:

- Reach: 13,800
- Profile visits: 510

Engagement:

- Saves: 61
- Shares: 28
- Comments: 33
- DMs started: 21

Inquiries:

- WhatsApp inquiries: 24

Conversions:

- Orders: 8
- Conversion rate: $8 \div 24 = 33\%$
- Revenue: 340,000
- Average order value: 42,500

Repeat:

- Repeat customers: 3
- Referrals: 2

Learning:
Customer stories increased inquiries, but conversion rate stayed the same. That means the sales chat needs improvement next.

Next weekly experiment:
Improve inquiry handling: use order summary + 2-option pricing menu.

This is how I grow with calm, week by week.

12) The simplest way to track in a notebook (if you hate digital tools)

If you do not want spreadsheets, do this:

One page per week.

Write:
Week of: _____

Traffic: _____
Engagement: _____
Inquiries: _____
Conversions: _____
Repeat: _____

Actions I did:

- Posts:
- Stories:
- Follow-ups:
- Broadcast:
- Collaborations:

One win:
One problem:
One change next week:

That is enough.

13) Practice: choose key metrics, track weekly, link results back to actions

Now we do the chapter practice.

Practice Step 1: Choose your key metrics (pick your "must track" list)

Start with these five:

Traffic:
Profile visits (or reach)

Engagement:
Saves + shares (combine them if needed)

Inquiries:
Number of serious inquiries (WhatsApp/DM)

Conversions:
Number of orders + conversion rate

Repeat:
Number of repeat customers

If you can add two more, add:
Revenue and on-time delivery rate

Practice Step 2: Set a weekly tracking time

Choose one day and time.

Example:
Sunday evening.
Monday morning.

The day matters less than consistency.

Practice Step 3: Track weekly for 8 weeks without quitting
Do not expect perfection in two weeks.

Tracking is a habit, and habits need time.

Your goal is not to look good.
Your goal is to learn the truth.

Practice Step 4: Link results back to actions
Every week, write:

These actions caused these results.

Then choose one change to test next week.

This is how evidence becomes growth.

14) The final lesson: measurement makes you peaceful and sharp
When I track my results, I stop being ruled by feelings.

I stop panicking when one day is quiet.
I stop celebrating too early when one post does well.
I stop changing everything at once.

Instead, I become steady.

I run my business like a system:
I act, I measure, I adjust, I repeat.

That is how small businesses become strong businesses.

Next, we move to Chapter Eleven, where we will talk about scaling and sustainable growth, meaning how I expand without breaking quality, trust, and my personal peace.

Chapter Eleven: Adapting and Evolving

If you build an online business and expect the ground to stay still, you will suffer.

Platforms change.
Algorithms change.
Prices shift.
Customers move.
Trends rise and die.
New competitors arrive.
Old tactics stop working.
Something that brought sales last month suddenly feels quiet this month.

This is not a crisis. This is the nature of the digital world.

The mistake many entrepreneurs make is emotional. They treat every change like an emergency. They panic, change everything, and then feel even more confused because they cannot tell what actually worked.

I learned a different way.

I stay relevant by learning fast and adjusting without panic. I keep my business steady by testing small changes, reading feedback, and making decisions based on evidence, not fear.

In this chapter, I will show you how I adapt when platforms change, trends shift, and new competitors appear. You will build a lightweight testing habit where you change one thing at a time, and you will build a feedback system that pulls information from customers, platform data, and sales. Then you will practice one small experiment per week, keeping what works and dropping what doesn't.

This is how a small business remains alive for years, not weeks.

1) The mindset: stability is not refusing change, stability is managing change

Some people think stability means doing the same thing forever.

That is not stability. That is stubbornness.

Real stability means:
I can change without breaking.

A stable business can adjust its message, its content format, its pricing communication, its platform emphasis, and its offer structure without losing its identity.

Identity is what stays.
Methods are what change.

So I hold my identity tightly:
My promise.
My values.
My quality standard.
My customer respect.

But I hold methods lightly:
Which platform I use most.
Which content format I publish.
Which hook style performs.
Which payment method is easiest.
Which delivery approach is safest.

This mindset removes panic.

If you think methods are your identity, every platform change feels like an attack.

But if your identity is deeper than the platform, you stay calm.

2) Why panic destroys learning

Panic makes you change too many variables at once.

You start doing all of this in one week:
New platform
New offer
New pricing
New content style
New posting time
New branding
New messaging tone
New link structure

Then you look at results and you cannot tell what caused what.

So you become dependent on luck.

If results improve, you assume all changes worked.
If results drop, you assume you are cursed or the platform hates you.

The truth is simpler:
You removed your ability to learn.

Learning requires controlled change.

That is why I use one change at a time.

3) What I teach: how I stay relevant when the world shifts
I stay relevant through five behaviors:

I monitor signals, not feelings.
I refresh skills deliberately.
I stay close to customers.
I watch competitors without copying them.
I test small changes weekly.

Let's go through each one.

Behavior 1: I monitor signals, not feelings
Feelings are unstable.

Signals are measurable.

Signals include:
Reach and profile visits
Saves and shares
DMs and WhatsApp inquiries
Conversion rate
Repeat customers
Complaints and returns.
Customer questions that keep repeating

When signals change, I pay attention.

If reach drops by 30% over three weeks, I do not panic.
I ask:
What changed in my posting frequency?
What format is being pushed now?
Is my audience shifting?
Are my hooks weak?
Did I stop showing proof?
Did I become inconsistent?

Signals guide questions.
Questions guide experiments.

Behavior 2: I refresh skills deliberately
Platforms reward competence.

When a platform shifts toward video, the entrepreneurs who learn simple video presentation win.
When a platform shifts toward carousels, the entrepreneurs who learn clean carousel teaching win.

I do not fight the trend. I learn the skill.

Skill refresh does not require a course marathon.

I choose one skill per month:
Better short video lighting
Better caption hooks
Better product photography
Better storytelling

Better offer structure
Better sales chat scripts

Then I practice it.

One skill per month compounds.

Behavior 3: I stay close to customers
Customers tell you what to do next if you listen.

Many entrepreneurs listen to gurus more than customers.

I do the opposite.

I pay attention to:

What customers ask before they buy
What customers complain about after they buy
What customers praise when they are happy
What customers request that I do not currently offer
What customers fear (scams, poor quality, delays)

This is gold.

If customers keep asking:
Do you deliver?
How long does it take?
What is the price?
Is it available?
Can I trust you?

Then your next improvements are obvious:
Clear delivery info
Clear timelines
Clear price ranges
Clear availability updates
More proof

Platforms may change, but customer fears remain similar.

Staying close to customer psychology keeps you relevant.

Behavior 4: I watch competitors without copying them
Competitors are signals too.

New competitors can be scary, but they can also teach you:

What customers are responding to
Which offers are rising
Which style is being adopted
Which pricing structures are common
Which service gaps exist

But copying is dangerous.

If you copy a competitor's voice, you lose identity.
If you copy a competitor's gimmicks, you attract the wrong audience.
If you copy a competitor's discounting, you destroy your margins.

So I watch competitors to learn:
Where the market is moving.

Then I respond in my own voice.

My goal is not to imitate.
My goal is to differentiate with quality and clarity.

Behavior 5: I test small changes weekly
This is the core.

Testing is how I stay relevant without gambling.

I run one small experiment per week.

Not ten experiments.
One.

Because one experiment gives clean learning.

4) What you build: a lightweight testing habit (one change at a time)

Now we build your testing habit.

A testing habit has five parts:

Baseline
Hypothesis
One change
One measurement window
Decision

Step 1: Baseline (what is normal right now)
Before you test, know your baseline numbers.

Baseline examples:
Average weekly reach
Average weekly inquiries
Average weekly conversion rate
Average weekly orders
Average weekly repeat customers

You already built a scorecard in the last chapter. This is where it becomes powerful.

If you do not know your baseline, you cannot tell if an experiment worked.

Step 2: Hypothesis (what do I believe will happen)
A hypothesis is a simple prediction.

Example hypotheses:
If I post 2 customer stories per week, inquiries will rise.
If I add price ranges in captions, conversions will rise.
If I reply within 30 minutes, conversion rate will rise.
If I publish one reel per week, reach will rise.
If I send a weekly broadcast, repeat customers will rise.

Write it down.

Writing it forces clarity.

Step 3: One change (only one)
Choose one variable.

Examples of single-variable changes:
Change posting frequency (3 posts to 4 posts)
Change format (add one reel per week)
Change content mix (increase proof posts)
Change caption structure (stronger hook + one CTA)
Change sales script (order summary message)
Change follow-up sequence (4-message sequence)
Change offer packaging (3 tiers)
Change posting time (morning vs evening)

Only one.

This protects learning.

Step 4: One measurement window (one week is enough to start)
Most small experiments can run for one week.

Some require two weeks (especially if you post less frequently).

But start with one week. Then repeat if promising.

Step 5: Decision (keep, adjust, or drop)
After the week, decide:

Keep:
If results improved meaningfully and you can sustain it.

Adjust:
If results improved slightly but needs refinement.

Drop:
If results did not improve or created more stress than value.

The decision is what makes testing useful.

5) What you build: a feedback system (customers, platform data, sales)

Feedback is your navigation system.

Without feedback, you are driving blind.

Your feedback system should pull from three sources:

Customer feedback
Platform data
Sales data

Let's build each.

A) Customer feedback system
I collect customer feedback through:

After-delivery check-in messages
Short questions:
What did you like most?
What should I improve?
What made you choose me?
What nearly stopped you from buying?

I also collect "silent feedback":
Questions customers keep repeating
Where customers get confused
Where customers hesitate
What objections keep appearing

I record these in a simple note weekly.

Customer feedback tells you what to improve next.

B) Platform data system
Platform data tells you:
What content is getting noticed, saved, shared, and clicked.

I watch:
Reach
Profile visits
Saves and shares
Comments
DMs started
Link clicks

I do not worship these numbers. I use them as signals.

If saves are high, the content is valuable.
If shares are high, the content is resonating.
If profile visits are high, people are curious.
If DMs are low, the call to action is weak or trust is not complete.

Platform data tells you what content to repeat and what to improve.

C) Sales data system
Sales data tells you the truth.

Sometimes engagement rises but sales fall.

That means the audience is not the right audience or your offer is unclear.

Sometimes reach drops but sales remain stable.

That means your relationship base is strong.

Sales data includes:
Inquiries
Conversion rate
Orders
Revenue
Repeat customers
Referrals
Refunds and complaints

Sales data tells you what matters most:
Is the business stable?

6) The weekly experiment engine: what to test (practical list)

Many entrepreneurs freeze because they do not know what to test.

Here is a practical list of experiments you can rotate through over 12 weeks.

Content experiments
Test 2 customer stories per week.
Test 1 behind-the-scenes reel per week.
Test one educational carousel per week.
Test posting at a different time.
Test shorter captions with one CTA.
Test one "how to order" post pinned weekly.

Engagement experiments
Test replying within 30 minutes for 5 days.
Test commenting on 10 relevant posts daily.
Test asking one question in stories daily for a week.
Test one collaboration feature swap.

Sales process experiments
Test a 3-option pricing menu.
Test an order summary message.
Test a deposit system for bookings.
Test a milestone update routine.
Test a follow-up sequence for all deliveries.

Offer experiments
Test bundling (bundle A vs single item).
Test a limited weekly slot system.
Test a new package tier (basic/standard/premium).
Test a "VIP list" for priority booking.

Retention experiments
Test a weekly broadcast message.
Test asking for reviews after delivery.
Test a small loyalty reward after 3 purchases.
Test a referral reward.

Pick one experiment per week.

Do not test everything at once.

7) How I avoid being late to trends without chasing trends
Trends can be useful, but they can also distract.

My rule:
I do not chase trends that do not match my customer.

I ask:
Is this trend used by my buyers?
Can I adapt it to my brand voice?
Does it help trust, proof, or clarity?
Can I do it consistently?

If yes, I adapt it.
If no, I ignore it.

Many trends are entertainment trends, not buying trends.

Your business is not a comedy channel.

You can be human, but you must stay aligned with buying behavior.

8) How I respond when a platform changes
Let's talk about platform shifts, because this is where panic happens.

When a platform changes, I do three things:

I observe for two weeks.
I keep posting consistently.
I run small format experiments.

I do not disappear.

Disappearing is the worst response to change.

If reach drops, I check:
Did the platform start pushing a different format?
Did my content mix become too offer-heavy?
Am I showing proof often enough?
Are my hooks weak?

Then I test:
Add one reel per week.
Add more proof posts.
Tighten hook lines.
Add clearer CTAs.

I let the data speak.

9) How I handle new competitors without fear

Competitors are normal.

If there are no competitors, the market may be too small.

When competitors appear, I strengthen my differentiation.

Differentiation is not bragging.
Differentiation is clarity.

I differentiate by:

Clear standards (quality proof)
Clear process (how I work)
Clear communication (fast replies and updates)
Clear identity (story and values)
Reliable delivery
Customer care

A competitor can copy your product.
A competitor cannot easily copy your reputation.

So I invest in reputation.

Reputation is a long-term asset.

10) Practice: run one small experiment per week
Now we do the practice.

You will run one small experiment per week.

Here is the structure you will use.

Weekly Experiment Template (copy)
Week of: _____

Baseline:
Reach: ____
Inquiries: ____
Orders: ____
Conversion rate: ____
Repeat customers: ____

Hypothesis:
If I _____, then _____ will increase/decrease.

Experiment (one change only):
This week I will _____.

Actions:
How many times I did it: _____

Results:
Reach: ____
Inquiries: ____
Orders: ____
Conversion rate: ____
Repeat customers: ____

Decision:
Keep / Adjust / Drop

Notes:
What I learned:
What I will do next week:

Do this every week.

After 8 weeks, your business becomes smarter.
After 24 weeks, your business becomes strong.
After one year, you will look back and realize you stopped guessing.

11) Keep what works, drop what doesn't: the discipline of refinement

The most important part of evolution is not trying new things.

It is removing what does not work.

Most businesses carry dead weight:
Posting content that never converts
Spending time on platforms that do not send buyers
Offering services that attract the wrong customers
Discounting too often
Arguing with customers
Overcomplicating ordering

Refinement means:
Stop doing low-return work.
Double down on what produces outcomes.

This is how small businesses scale without burning out.

12) The final lesson: adapt with calm, evolve with evidence

The world will keep changing.

If you treat that as a threat, you will live in panic.
If you treat that as normal, you will build a stable system.

My method is simple:
One change at a time.
One week at a time.
Measure.
Learn.
Keep what works.
Drop what doesn't.

That is how I stay relevant without losing my identity.

And that is how you build a business that survives platform shifts, trend waves, and competitor noise.

Next, we move into the final chapters where we connect measurement and adaptation to sustainable scaling, meaning how to grow your output, your team, and your income without sacrificing quality, trust, or your personal peace.

Chapter Twelve: Beyond the Basics

When I first started building an online business, the early wins felt exciting. A few inquiries. A few orders. People sharing my work. Customers saying, "I saw your post." That stage matters because it proves the business can breathe online.

But there is another stage that decides whether you remain a small hustle or become a real enterprise.

That stage is expansion.

Expansion is not just more followers. Expansion is not just more posts. Expansion is not just being "busy." Expansion is when the business grows beyond the basics and begins to stand on systems. It becomes reliable enough to handle more customers, enter new markets, and produce results even when I am tired, traveling, or dealing with life.

This chapter is about how I grow from "online presence" to "real expansion." That means scaling systems, entering new markets, strengthening operations, and building a brand people can carry beyond me. You will build a growth plan that includes new products, partnerships, improved fulfillment, and a stronger brand community. Then you will build a delegation plan for tasks you should not keep doing alone. Finally, you will choose one expansion path and build the system behind it before you chase the next shiny idea.

This is where entrepreneurship becomes serious.

1) The difference between growth and expansion

Growth is when you do more and earn more.

Expansion is when you become capable of more without breaking.

A business can grow without expanding. Many entrepreneurs are proof of this. They increase sales, but everything still depends on their hands, their phone, their mood, and their personal energy. If they stop, everything stops.

That is growth without expansion.

Expansion is when the business can continue even when I am not doing everything.

Expansion comes from four things:

Systems that reduce chaos
Operations that protect quality
Market strategy that increases reach
Brand strength that creates loyalty beyond the founder

If you want a business that lasts, you must move from "being present online" to building these four.

2) The expansion mindset: stop thinking like a worker, start thinking like a builder

In the early stage, I do most things myself. That is normal.

But if I stay in that stage too long, I become the bottleneck.

The business becomes a job that I created for myself, not a machine that supports my life.

So I adopt a builder mindset.

A builder asks different questions:

How do I make this repeatable?
How do I reduce mistakes?
How do I shorten delivery time without lowering quality?
How do I make customers feel safe even when I am busy?
How do I document what I do so someone else can help?
How do I scale trust, not only sales?

Builder questions lead to systems.

Systems are what allow expansion.

3) What I teach: how I go from online presence to real expansion

Real expansion has five moves:

Scale what already works
Strengthen operations before entering new markets
Enter new markets carefully and deliberately
Build partnerships that multiply reach
Build a brand community that can live beyond me

Let's unpack these.

Move 1: Scale what already works (not what looks exciting)

Most entrepreneurs skip this step.

They have one winning product, and instead of scaling it, they chase new ideas.

New ideas are seductive, but scaling a proven offer is usually the fastest and safest path.

So I start expansion by asking:

What product or service brings the most profit with the least stress?
Which customers are easiest to serve and most respectful?
Which channel brings the most serious buyers?
Which process is already smooth and repeatable?

Then I scale that.

Scaling means:
More capacity
More consistency
More speed

More proof
More availability

It does not mean random new offerings.

Move 2: Strengthen operations (because growth breaks weak businesses)

When orders increase, weak operations collapse.

Common signs of weak operations:
Late delivery
Wrong orders
Lost messages
Confusing pricing
No inventory control
Poor packaging
Inconsistent quality
Refunds and arguments
Stress and burnout

If you want expansion, operations must become strong.

Operations are the invisible engine.

Move 3: Enter new markets carefully (not blindly)

Entering new markets can mean:
A new neighborhood
A new city
A new country
A new platform
A new customer segment (corporate, wholesale, resellers)

New markets bring new complexity:
Different tastes
Different pricing expectations
Different payment methods
Different delivery logistics
Different competition

So I enter new markets with testing and systems, not hope.

Move 4: Build partnerships (the fastest way to multiply reach)
Partnerships are leverage.

Instead of me doing all marketing alone, partnerships allow other businesses to bring customers to me, and I bring customers to them.

A strong partnership is built on:
Shared audience
Non-competing offers
Mutual benefit
Clear referral rules
Consistent quality

Partnerships reduce marketing cost and increase trust.

Move 5: Build a brand people can carry beyond me
If everything depends on my personal presence, my brand is fragile.

A strong brand can be carried by staff, partners, resellers, and customers.

That kind of brand needs:
Clear standards
Clear voice and tone
Clear promises
Clear visual identity
Clear processes
Clear customer experience

When these are documented, the brand can expand without losing itself.

4) The expansion map: the four pillars I strengthen
To move beyond the basics, I strengthen four pillars:

Offer
Operations

Distribution
Community

A) Offer: what I sell and how I package it
Expansion often starts with improving the offer.

I use these offer strategies:

Add tiers:
Basic, Standard, Premium

Add bundles:
Buy X + get Y

Add recurring:
Monthly package, subscription, maintenance plan, repeat delivery

Add corporate:
Business uniforms, corporate gifting, office packages

Add wholesale:
Reseller bundles, bulk pricing

Expansion becomes easier when the offer is packaged for scale.

B) Operations: how I fulfill with consistency
Operations include:
Order intake process
Pricing and quoting system
Inventory and supplies
Production workflow
Quality control checkpoints
Packaging and delivery
Customer updates
Problem resolution

Operations are where trust is built.

C) Distribution: how the product reaches customers
Distribution includes:
Delivery network
Pickup points
Shipping system
Digital delivery (for digital products)
Partner outlets

A business can have a great offer and still fail because distribution is weak.

D) Community: how customers stay connected
Community includes:
WhatsApp broadcast
Customer group
Email list
Social media community
VIP customer list
Referral network

Community creates retention and referrals.

5) What you build: a growth plan
Now we build your growth plan.

A growth plan is not a long document. It is a clear one-page plan you can execute over 90 days.

Your growth plan will cover:

New products (or improved offer)
Partnerships
Improved fulfillment
Stronger brand community

Here is the structure.

The 90-Day Growth Plan (copy and fill)

A) Growth focus (choose one)
My main growth focus for the next 90 days is:

- scale my best-selling offer
or
- enter one new market
or
- build a partnership channel
or
- improve fulfillment speed and reliability
or
- build a stronger community and retention loop

Pick one.

B) Offer improvements
What will I improve or add?
Examples:
Add premium tier
Add bundles
Add corporate package
Add a new product line connected to the best seller

C) Partnerships
Which partners will I approach?
Examples:
Photographers
Event planners
Retail outlets
Influencers with aligned audience
Local businesses serving the same customers

What is the partnership model?
Referral fee
Feature swap
Bundle offer
Shared promotion

D) Fulfillment improvements
What will I fix in operations?
Examples:
Order summary script
Production checklist
Quality check routine
Packaging standard
Delivery update routine

E) Brand community improvements
What community system will I build?
Examples:
Weekly broadcast
VIP list
Customer referral system
Monthly customer spotlight
Feedback collection routine

F) Weekly actions (minimums)
What are my weekly minimum actions to execute this plan?
Examples:
One partner outreach per week
One system improvement per week
Three posts per week aligned with offer
One broadcast message per week
Follow-up messages sent after delivery

This plan gives direction without overwhelm.

6) What you build: a delegation plan (tasks you should not keep doing alone)

Expansion requires a hard truth.

If I keep doing everything, I will cap the business.

Delegation is not luxury. Delegation is capacity.

Delegation means:
Someone else does the task with clear instructions, so I can focus on the founder tasks.

Founder tasks are:
Quality standards
Brand voice
Offer strategy
Customer experience design
Partnership building
System improvement
High-value relationships

Everything else can be delegated.

Step 1: Identify tasks that drain me and do not need my talent

Common tasks to delegate:

Basic customer replies (using scripts)
Scheduling posts
Editing photos and videos
Packaging
Delivery coordination
Inventory tracking
Bookkeeping and receipts
Order logging
Customer follow-up messages
Basic design repetition tasks
Data entry for weekly scorecard

If the task is repetitive and rule-based, it is a delegation candidate.

Step 2: Choose delegation levels (not all delegation is the same)

There are three levels:

Helper:
Does simple tasks with supervision.

Operator:
Runs a process reliably (packaging, delivery coordination, follow-up routine).

Manager:
Oversees people and systems (later stage).

In early expansion, you usually need a Helper or Operator first.

Step 3: Create simple SOPs (standard operating procedures)
An SOP is a one-page instruction.

It answers:
What is the task?
What is the standard?
What are the steps?
What does "done" look like?
What mistakes must be avoided?

If you want people to help without breaking quality, you need SOPs.

Step 4: Build a training loop
Training is not one day.

Training is:
Show once
Watch them do it
Correct
Repeat

Then you trust gradually.

Delegation is how the business becomes bigger than the founder.

7) Scaling systems: what must become "systemized" first
If you are limited in time and energy, prioritize systemizing the areas that protect trust:

Order intake
Pricing clarity
Production workflow
Quality control
Delivery updates
Customer follow-up
Proof collection (testimonials)

These systems reduce errors and increase repeat business.

The Order Intake System
Goal: no lost orders, no confusion.

Tools:
Order summary template
Labeling system
Order log

The Pricing System
Goal: customers understand cost and stop wasting time.

Tools:
2 to 3 option pricing menu
Clear price ranges
Clear add-on pricing

The Production Workflow
Goal: consistent quality under higher volume.

Tools:
Checklist
Quality checkpoints
Time estimates per product/service

The Delivery Update System
Goal: customer confidence.

Tools:
Milestone updates (confirmed, started, packaging, out for delivery, delivered)

The Follow-up System
Goal: retention and referrals.

Tools:
4-message follow-up sequence
Review request routine
Broadcast invite

If you systemize these, expansion becomes safer.

8) Entering new markets: the safest paths for expansion

New markets can be exciting, but they can also kill a business if you rush.

Here are safe expansion paths:

Path 1: Expand within the same customer type
Same product, more capacity, better delivery.

This is the simplest and safest.

Path 2: Expand through partnerships
Instead of entering a new city alone, partner with someone who already has trust there.

Path 3: Expand through resellers or agents
Train a reseller to sell your products with your standards.

Path 4: Expand through digital products or services
If you can create something that delivers digitally, it can scale faster.

Path 5: Expand through corporate and bulk clients
One corporate client can be equal to many individual clients.

Each path requires systems.

Choose one.

9) Strengthening operations: how I protect quality while scaling

As volume rises, quality is the first thing that gets attacked.

So I protect quality through:

Standards
Checklists
Time buffers
Supplier consistency
Clear customer expectations
Correction policy

Standards
Define what "good" looks like.

Example:
Stitching must be clean.
Packaging must be neat.
Delivery must be on time.
Communication must be respectful.
Updates must be predictable.

Checklists
Checklists reduce mistakes.

A checklist is not for beginners only. It is for professionals who want consistency.

Time buffers
If you promise unrealistic timelines, you create stress and errors.

So I build small buffers into delivery timelines.

Supplier consistency
Scaling often fails because suppliers are inconsistent.

So I stabilize my supply chain before I scale marketing.

Clear expectations
If customers expect magic, they become unhappy.

So I communicate:
What is included
Timeline
Payment terms
Delivery terms
Adjustment policy

Clarity reduces conflict.

10) Building a brand community that can grow beyond me
This is the long-term expansion engine.

A community makes your brand durable.

Community is how your customers become your marketing.

To build community beyond the founder, I create:

A clear brand message customers can repeat
A customer spotlight habit
A broadcast rhythm
A referral culture
A shared identity around quality and respect

If customers feel proud to be associated with your brand, they will carry it.

People share what makes them feel good.

So I ask:
What feeling does my brand give?
Confidence?
Clean professionalism?
Peace of mind?
Belonging?

Then I build content and service around that feeling.

11) Practice: choose one expansion path and build the system behind it

Now we do the chapter practice.

Your practice has one rule:

Choose one expansion path.
Build the system behind it.
Do not chase the next shiny idea until the system works.

Here is how to do it.

Step 1: Choose one expansion path (pick one)
Option A: scale the best-selling offer (more capacity, stronger operations)
Option B: enter a new market (new area or customer segment)
Option C: build a partnership channel (referrals and bundles)
Option D: build a reseller/agent model
Option E: build a community-led retention system (broadcast, VIP list, referral loop)

Pick one.

Step 2: Identify the system you must build first
If you chose A (scale best seller):
Build order intake system + production checklist + delivery update routine.

If you chose B (new market):
Build market test plan + delivery method + local partner or pickup system + proof for that market.

If you chose C (partnership channel):
Build partner pitch script + referral rules + partner onboarding kit + tracking system.

If you chose D (reseller model):
Build product standard guide + reseller pricing + training + order and delivery process.

If you chose E (community retention):
Build weekly broadcast plan + follow-up sequence + review system + referral reward.

Step 3: Build the system in writing (simple documents)
This is the real work.

Write:
Scripts
Checklists
SOPs
Pricing menus
Partner rules

When it is written, it can be repeated and delegated.

Step 4: Run it for 30 days before adding another expansion idea
Expansion is not a sprint.

The temptation is to add more and more.
But stability comes from making one system reliable first.

A business that can do one thing well at scale is stronger than a business that tries ten things poorly.

12) The final lesson: expansion is discipline, not excitement

The internet makes everything look fast.

But real expansion is built slowly, with discipline.

Systems first.
Operations next.
Partnerships and markets after.
Community always.

If you follow this order, you do not just grow.

You expand.

And when you expand, your brand becomes bigger than you, while still carrying your standards and your identity.

That is the goal.

In the next section, we move into the closing part of the book, where we pull everything together into a practical expansion roadmap, showing how to plan the next 6 to 12 months with calm, structure, and measurable progress.

IMPLEMENTATION SPRINTS (Work sections readers can follow)

The biggest difference between people who "learn business" and people who build a business is simple.

Learners collect ideas.
Builders execute in cycles.

That is why I love sprints.

A sprint is a short, focused period where you do the most important work, measure results, and make adjustments. Sprints keep you from drifting. They also protect you from perfectionism, because you are not trying to build everything at once. You are building one layer at a time.

In this section, I give you three sprints you can follow exactly:

The 7-day setup sprint
The 30-day consistency sprint
The 90-day growth sprint

These sprints are designed for real life, including places with unstable connectivity, limited budgets, and limited time. They work for service businesses, product businesses, local shops, freelancers, and online creators. You will notice one theme in all three sprints: simple steps, repeated consistently.

You do not need to do everything. You need to do the right things in the right order.

The 7-Day Setup Sprint
(Offer, audience, platform, first posts)

This sprint is about clarity and momentum. The goal is not perfection. The goal is to set foundations, publish your first real content, and create a working path for customers to reach you.

At the end of 7 days, you should have:
A clear offer
A clear audience description
One main platform chosen
A basic profile that looks trustworthy
A simple ordering path (how customers contact and buy)
Your first set of posts published
A basic follow-up habit started

If you do this sprint properly, you stop being invisible and you stop being confused.

Day 1: Define your offer (what you sell, who it is for, why it matters)

Today is about turning your business into one clear sentence.

If you cannot describe your offer clearly, customers will not buy.

I define my offer using this structure:

I help (who) get (result) using (what I deliver) so they can (benefit).

Examples:
I help busy professionals look sharp using custom shirts delivered on time so they feel confident at work.
I help small businesses grow online using content and simple systems so they get consistent inquiries.
I help families celebrate events using cakes designed for their occasion so they feel proud and remembered.

Now define your offer in plain language.

Then define your "offer components":
What exactly do you deliver?
What are the options?
What is the usual price range?
How long does it take?
How do people order?

Deliverable for Day 1:
Write your offer sentence.
Write 3 bullet points of what you deliver.
Write your starting price or price range.
Write your typical timeline.

Day 2: Define your audience (stop chasing everyone)

Many businesses lose money because they try to sell to everyone.

If you sell to everyone, you speak to no one.

Today, I build an "ideal customer page."

I write:

Who they are (age range, lifestyle, work type, location)
What they want (results, feelings, outcomes)
What they fear (scams, delays, poor quality, embarrassment)
What they value (speed, trust, status, affordability, custom)
What makes them trust (proof, reviews, brand stability, clarity)
Where they spend time online (platforms, groups, creators)
What they say when they are ready to buy (their language)

This page becomes my marketing compass.

Deliverable for Day 2:
Write one ideal customer profile.
Write 10 words or phrases they use.
Write 5 questions they often ask before buying.

Day 3: Choose your main platform and set up your "home base"

Today, I decide where I will build consistency.

Pick one main platform based on:
Where your audience already is
Where your product can be shown clearly
Where you can be consistent

For many businesses:
Instagram works well for visuals.
WhatsApp works well for direct selling and local community.
Facebook works well for local groups and community markets.
LinkedIn works well for professional services and corporate clients.
TikTok works well for reach if you can do video consistently.

You can use more than one platform later, but in this sprint you choose one main platform.

Then set up a simple "home base."
Home base can be:
A one-page website
A store page
A pinned post with ordering steps
A WhatsApp Business catalog

The goal is: customers can see proof and understand how to order even if you are busy.

Deliverable for Day 3:
Main platform chosen.
Profile updated (photo, name, bio, promise, contact).
Home base set (catalog or one page or pinned post).

Day 4: Build your first content pillars and post templates
Today is about content structure.

I do not post randomly. I post in pillars.

Choose three pillars:
Proof (customer stories, testimonials, results)
Process (behind the scenes, quality checks)
Education (tips, mistakes, how to choose)

Then create simple post templates for each pillar.

Proof post template:
Customer result + short story + proof + call to action

Process post template:
Behind the scenes + what standard you keep + why it matters + call to action

Education post template:
One tip + why it matters + simple steps + call to action

Deliverable for Day 4:
Write 3 post drafts (one for each pillar).
Collect 6 to 9 photos or videos you can post.

Day 5: Publish your first two posts and practice engagement

Today, I start showing up publicly.

Post 1: Proof or process (show real work or real standards)
Post 2: Education (teach something simple customers care about)

Then do engagement:

Reply to every comment.
Message back any inquiries fast.
Comment on 10 posts where your audience is active.

Deliverable for Day 5:
Two posts published.
10 meaningful comments left.
All messages replied.

Day 6: Create your basic sales flow (inquiry to order)

Today is about making it easy for people to buy.

Create three scripts:
Inquiry script
Pricing script
Order confirmation script

Inquiry script:
Thanks for reaching out. What do you want, when do you need it, and what is your budget range?

Pricing script:
Based on your request, the range is ____. Option A is ____, option B is ____. Which one fits you?

Order confirmation script:
To confirm, please send payment/deposit to ____. Once confirmed, delivery is ____. I will update you at key stages.

Deliverable for Day 6:
Scripts written and saved as quick replies.
One catalog or price menu created (even if basic).

Day 7: Publish again, invite action, and set the weekly rhythm

Today is about making your work repeatable.

Publish one more post (proof or customer story if possible).

Then post a clear "how to order" message.
Make it easy:
Message me
Share your deadline
Pick an option
Pay to confirm

Then create your weekly minimums.

Weekly minimums (starter):
3 posts per week
Daily reply habit
One weekly review on Sunday
One weekly broadcast message if you use WhatsApp

Deliverable for Day 7:
One post published.

Ordering steps posted.
Weekly minimum plan written.

At the end of 7 days, you are no longer guessing. You have a working foundation.

The 30-Day Consistency Sprint
(Content rhythm, engagement, basic tracking)

This sprint is where most people quit. That is why this sprint creates winners.

Consistency is not glamorous, but it is powerful.

The goal of 30 days is to create rhythm:
A content rhythm you can sustain
An engagement rhythm that builds relationships
A tracking rhythm that shows you what works

At the end of 30 days, you should have:
A stable posting routine
A stable engagement routine
A basic weekly scorecard
A clearer message based on real feedback
More trust and more inquiries than before

Week 1: Build your rhythm and protect your time
Do not aim for daily posts if that will break you.

Aim for a rhythm you can keep.

I recommend:
3 posts per week
Stories most days (short updates)
Daily engagement (30 minutes total)

Choose your posting days.
Example:
Monday, Wednesday, Friday

Choose your engagement windows.
Example:
15 minutes in the morning, 15 minutes in the evening

Then write your content plan for the week:
One proof post
One process post
One education post

Deliverable for Week 1:
Posting days fixed.
Engagement windows fixed.
3 posts published.

Week 2: Improve your message and your call to action

Now that you are posting, you will see which posts get response.

This week, you tighten your message.

What I change first:
Hooks
Clarity
Ordering steps

Write stronger first lines.
Use simpler captions.
Add one call to action in every post:
Message me with your deadline.
Reply with "ORDER."
Ask for a quote.

Also, start collecting proof:
Ask customers for short feedback lines.
Ask for photos.
Save them in a folder.

Deliverable for Week 2:
3 posts published with clear CTAs.
5 pieces of proof collected (screenshots, feedback, photos).

Week 3: Build your engagement system and your community habits

This week, you focus on relationships.

Daily:
Reply fast.
Ask good questions.
Comment where your audience is active.

Weekly:
Feature one customer story.
Ask one question in stories or posts.
Do one collaboration touch (feature swap or partner mention).

If you have WhatsApp:
Start a weekly broadcast message.

Deliverable for Week 3:
Engagement done daily.
1 customer feature posted.
1 broadcast message sent.

Week 4: Basic tracking and a simple weekly review

Now you stop operating by feelings.

Track five metrics weekly:
Traffic (profile visits or reach)
Engagement (saves and shares)
Inquiries (WhatsApp/DM serious messages)
Conversions (orders)
Repeat customers

Write them every week.

Then review:
What improved?
What dropped?
What action caused it?
What will I test next?

Deliverable for Week 4:
Scorecard completed weekly.
One weekly experiment chosen for next month.

At the end of 30 days, you should feel clearer. You will also have proof, momentum, and data.

The 90-Day Growth Sprint
(SEO, partnerships, customer retention, experiments)

This sprint is where your business begins to feel real.

The goal is not only to post and engage. The goal is to grow through systems:

SEO and search visibility
Partnerships and collaborations
Customer retention and loyalty
Weekly experiments and improvement

At the end of 90 days, you should have:
A stronger content system
A simple SEO strategy (if you use a website or searchable platform)
At least 3 partnership relationships started
A retention system running (follow-ups, reviews, broadcast)
A weekly experiment habit built
A measurable increase in inquiries, conversions, or repeat customers

Month 1 (Days 1–30): Strengthen your foundation and start retention

In the first month, you do not chase expansion yet. You strengthen what you already built.

Focus areas:
Content rhythm (keep it consistent)
Sales scripts (improve conversion)
Retention (follow-up sequence)
Proof collection (reviews and testimonials)

Actions:
Use the 4-message follow-up sequence after every delivery.
Ask for reviews and testimonials weekly.
Send one broadcast message weekly.
Track weekly metrics.

Deliverable:
Retention system running.
Reviews collected.
Repeat customer rate beginning to rise.

Month 2 (Days 31-60): Add SEO and search visibility

SEO does not have to be complicated.

SEO means:
When people search for what you sell, they can find you.

SEO shows up in many places:
Google search
Instagram search
Facebook search
TikTok search
Marketplace search
Your website

This month, you build basic SEO habits:

Use consistent keywords in your bio and posts:
What you sell + location + audience

Examples:
Custom shirts in Nairobi
Event cakes in Juba
Phone repair in Chicago
Online business coaching for beginners

Create 5 evergreen posts that answer common questions:
How to order
Pricing guide

Delivery areas
Quality standards
Best options for different needs

If you have a website:
Create 3 pages or posts targeting common searches.

Deliverable:
Search-friendly profile.
Evergreen content published.
Website basics improved if applicable.

Month 3 (Days 61–90): Partnerships, experiments, and expansion signals

Now you add leverage.

Partnerships:
Reach out to one partner per week.
Offer a simple collaboration:
Feature swap
Bundle offer
Referral agreement

Experiments:
Run one small experiment per week.
One change at a time.

Examples:
Add 2 customer stories per week
Add one reel per week
Add pricing ranges in every caption
Reply within 30 minutes
Use a 3-option pricing menu

Retention:
Keep follow-ups.
Keep broadcast.
Keep collecting proof.

Deliverable:
At least 3 partnerships started.
At least 8 experiments run.
Clear data on what improved growth.

The sprint rule that keeps you from chasing shiny ideas
Here is the rule I live by:

Do not expand until your basics are consistent.
Do not chase new platforms until one platform is working.
Do not add new products until your best offer has a system.
Do not hire help until you have simple instructions.

Sprints help you earn the right to expand.

A closing instruction from me to you
If you follow these sprints, you will stop feeling like you are "trying online business."

You will be building one.

Do not wait for confidence.
Confidence comes after repetition.

Do the 7 days.
Then do the 30 days.
Then do the 90 days.

And when you look back, you will see the truth:

You did not grow because you found a secret.
You grew because you built a system, one sprint at a time.

FIELD GUIDE APPENDICES (Copy-ready tools)

These appendices are designed to be copy-ready. I wrote them so you can paste them into a notebook, a Google Doc, a phone note, or a simple spreadsheet and start using them immediately. If you use them consistently, your business will feel more organized, more professional, and easier to grow.

Appendix A: Brand Identity Sheet Template (Copy-ready)

Use this to translate a real business into a clear online identity. Keep it short and truthful. Do not write what sounds nice. Write what you can actually deliver.

BRAND NAME:
BUSINESS TYPE (product/service):
LOCATION/SERVICE AREA:
PRIMARY PLATFORM:
SECONDARY PLATFORM (optional):

1. Purpose (why this business exists)
   My business exists to:

---

2. Promise (what customers can expect every time)
   Customers can expect:

---

3. Target audience (who I serve best)
   I serve:

---

4. Core values (3 to 5 values, plain language)
   Value 1:
   Value 2:
   Value 3:

Value 4 (optional):
   Value 5 (optional):
5. Brand voice (how I sound when I write and speak)
   Choose 3 to 5 words:
   Example options: warm, direct, respectful, practical, professional, bold, calm, friendly
   My brand voice is:

---

6. Tone boundaries (what I will never sound like)
   I will never sound:

---

7. Brand story (short version: 3 to 6 sentences)
   Where I started:
   What I believe:
   What I make/do:
   Why it matters:

---

8. Visual identity (make it simple and consistent)
   Primary colors (2 to 3):
   Secondary colors (1 to 2):
   Font style (serif/sans/handwritten):
   Photo style (bright/dark, clean/busy, studio/natural):
   Background style (plain, textured, lifestyle, etc.):
9. Signature content pillars (pick 3)
   Proof (customer results):
   Process (behind the scenes):
   Education (tips/how-to):
   Story (meaning and origin):
   Community (customer features):
   My 3 pillars:
10. _____
11. _____
12. _____

13. Brand keywords (words people should associate with me)
    Example: reliable, clean finishing, on-time, premium, simple, affordable
    My keywords:

---

11. About page outline (if you have a website or pinned post)
    Who I am:
    Who I serve:
    What I offer:
    How to order:
    What makes me different:

---

12. Customer experience standard (non-negotiables)
    Response time goal:
    Delivery time promise:
    Quality standards:
    Problem resolution policy:

Appendix B: Ideal Customer Sheet Template (Copy-ready)

You cannot market to everyone. Use this sheet to define the right customer clearly.

IDEAL CUSTOMER NAME (you can give them a name):
AGE RANGE:
LOCATION:
JOB/LIFESTYLE:
BUDGET LEVEL (low/medium/high):
MAIN PLATFORM(S) THEY USE:

1. What they want (results and feelings)
   They want:

2. What they fear (before buying)
   They fear:

3. What frustrates them about other sellers
   They hate:

4. What makes them trust a seller
   They trust:

5. Their buying triggers (what makes them decide now)
   They buy when:

6. Their common questions
   Question 1:
   Question 2:
   Question 3:
   Question 4:
   Question 5:
7. Their language (words they use)
   Write 10 phrases:
8.
9.
10.
11.
12.
13.
14.
15.
16.

17.
18. Objections (why they hesitate)
    Objection 1:
    Objection 2:
    Objection 3:
19. How my business answers those objections
    Answer 1:
    Answer 2:
    Answer 3:
20. Best offer for them (what I should sell them first)
    Starter offer:

Appendix C: Content Calendar Template (Copy-ready)

This template is built for consistency. It is simple enough to maintain even with weak internet or a busy schedule.

CONTENT PILLARS (choose 3):
Pillar 1:
Pillar 2:
Pillar 3:

POSTING FREQUENCY:
Posts per week:
Stories per week:
Reels/videos per week (optional):

WEEKLY THEMES (optional):
Week theme:
Example: back to work, wedding season, school season, new month

WEEKLY CALENDAR (fill each week)

MONDAY
Post type (proof/process/education/story):
Topic:

Media needed (photo/video):
CTA (what you want people to do):

TUESDAY
Stories topic:
Engagement task (comment/DM/follow-up):

WEDNESDAY
Post type:
Topic:
Media needed:
CTA:

THURSDAY
Stories topic:
Engagement task:

FRIDAY
Post type:
Topic:
Media needed:
CTA:

SATURDAY
Community/UGC post or broadcast message:
Offer/availability update:

SUNDAY
Weekly review + plan next week:
Scorecard update:
One experiment for next week:

Appendix D: Photo and Caption Checklist (Copy-ready)

Use this before you publish. It keeps your content clean and consistent.

PHOTO CHECKLIST

- Lighting is clear (not too dark, not too yellow)

- Main product is the focus (no clutter behind it)
- The photo tells one clear story (no confusion)
- Product details are visible (texture, finishing, quality)
- Background supports the product (simple and clean)
- At least one close-up shot included (if relevant)
- If it's a person, the pose looks natural and confident
- Photo is cropped for the platform (no important parts cut off)
- Brand style matches my usual feed look

CAPTION CHECKLIST

- First line is strong and relevant to the customer
- Caption is easy to read (short paragraphs)
- I explain benefit, not only features
- I include proof (customer result, standard, timeline, testimonial)
- I include one clear call to action (message me, order, ask for price)
- I avoid too many emojis or distractions (optional)
- I include location if relevant
- I include keywords customers search for (what + location)

CTA IDEAS (pick one)

- Message me your deadline and I'll guide you
- Reply "ORDER" and I'll send options
- Want the price list? Message me "PRICE"
- Which option would you choose, A or B?

Appendix E: Instagram Checklist (Copy-ready)

This checklist makes your profile and routine more professional.

PROFILE SETUP

- Profile photo is clear and consistent
- Username matches business name
- Bio includes what I sell + who it's for + location

- WhatsApp link or contact button works
- Highlights are organized (Prices, Reviews, How to Order, Delivery)
- 3 pinned posts:
    1. How to order
    2. Proof/testimonials
    3. Best seller or pricing guide

WEEKLY ROUTINE

- 3 posts per week (proof/process/education)
- Stories most days (updates, polls, behind the scenes)
- 30 minutes daily engagement (reply + comments)
- One customer feature per week
- One weekly review of results

CONTENT QUALITY

- Clear photos
- Short, direct captions
- One call to action per post
- Proof posted regularly (testimonials, results)

Appendix F: WhatsApp Group Rules and Welcome Message Templates (Copy-ready)

WhatsApp is a trust space. Rules protect trust.

WHATSAPP GROUP RULES (copy and edit)
Welcome to (Group Name). This group is for (purpose).

Rules:

1. No spam, no unrelated links, no forwarded chain messages.
2. Be respectful. No insults, tribal fights, or political arguments.
3. No posting other people's phone numbers without permission.
4. Keep messages relevant to the group purpose.

5. Admins may remove repeated offenders to protect the group.

Ordering:
To order, message the admin directly with:

- what you want
- your deadline
- your budget range

Posting rhythm:
Admins post (days or frequency). Keep notifications on if you want updates.

WELCOME MESSAGE TEMPLATE (copy)
Welcome to (Group Name). This group is for (purpose: updates, tips, customer stories, and weekly availability). I post (frequency). To order, message me directly with your deadline and what you want. Please follow the rules in the pinned message so the group stays useful and respectful. Quick question: are you here to learn, order, or both?

Appendix G: Twitter (X) Posting Rhythm Template (Copy-ready)

X is built on consistency. Treat posts like chapters of your brand story.

PROFILE BASICS

- Clear promise in bio (what I do, who I help)
- One link (WhatsApp, website, store page)
- Pinned post: "Start here" with ordering or service steps

POSTING RHYTHM (weekly)

- 5 short posts per week (one idea each)
- 2 threads per week (teaching or story)
- 10 replies per day (short, useful comments)

CONTENT MIX (rotate)

- Education (tips, mistakes)
- Proof (customer results)
- Process (how I work)
- Offer (availability, pricing, ordering)

THREAD TEMPLATE (copy)
Post 1: Hook (strong problem or truth)
Post 2: Why it matters
Post 3: Lesson 1
Post 4: Lesson 2
Post 5: Lesson 3
Post 6: Example/proof
Final post: CTA (follow/message/order)

Appendix H: LinkedIn Profile Checklist and Outreach Template (Copy-ready)

LINKEDIN PROFILE CHECKLIST

- Profile photo is professional and clear
- Headline states what I do + who I help + outcome
- About section includes:
    - who I help
    - what I do
    - proof/results
    - how to contact me
- Featured section includes proof (case study, testimonials, portfolio)
- Skills match what I want to be known for
- At least 1 recommendation requested or displayed (when possible)

OUTREACH TEMPLATE (Connection request)
Hello (Name). I saw your work in (context). I'm in (your business/industry) and I help (audience) with (outcome). Happy to connect.

FOLLOW-UP TEMPLATE (after they accept)
Thanks for connecting, (Name). Quick question: what kind of (product/service need) do you see most in your work right now? I'm always learning what people need so I can serve better.

PARTNERSHIP TEMPLATE (optional)
If you ever have clients who need (your service/product), I'd be happy to support them. I also refer clients to trusted partners. If you're open, we can test a simple referral partnership.

Appendix I: Customer Follow-up Scripts (Copy-ready)

INQUIRY SCRIPT
Thanks for reaching out. What do you want, when do you need it, and what is your budget range? I'll guide you with options.

PRICING SCRIPT
Based on your request, the range is ____ to ____. Option A is ____ (timeline). Option B is ____ (timeline). Which one fits you?

ORDER SUMMARY SCRIPT
Just confirming: you ordered ____ for ____ (deadline). Total price: ____. Delivery/pickup: ____. Correct?

PAYMENT RECEIVED SCRIPT
Payment received, thank you. Your order is confirmed. Next update by ____.

WORK STARTED UPDATE
Work started and everything is on schedule. Next update by ____.

PACKAGING UPDATE
Your order is packaged and ready. Delivery today between ____ and ____.

OUT FOR DELIVERY UPDATE
Out for delivery now. Rider contact: ____. Please keep your phone available.

DELIVERED MESSAGE
Delivered successfully. Thank you for trusting me.

AFTER-SALE CARE (Day 1–2)
How is everything so far? If you need any adjustment or support, tell me and I'll help.

FEEDBACK REQUEST (Day 3–5)
If you have one minute, what did you like most and what can I improve?

REVIEW REQUEST (Day 7–10)
If you're happy with it, could you leave a short review or feedback? It helps other customers trust my work. I appreciate it.

BROADCAST INVITE
I share weekly updates once a week. Want me to add you to my broadcast list?

PROBLEM-SOLVING SCRIPT
Thanks for telling me. I understand and I want to fix it. Can you share a photo or explain what feels wrong? Here are the options: (1) adjustment by _____, (2) replacement by _____, (3) refund/alternative solution _____. Which one works best for you?

Appendix J: Giveaway and User-Generated Content Plan Template (Copy-ready)

Giveaways and UGC work when they build trust, not when they attract freebie hunters.

GOAL (choose one)

- grow local awareness
- collect customer photos and testimonials
- increase inquiries
- launch a new offer

PRIZE (make it aligned with your ideal customer)
Prize:
Value:
Why it attracts buyers (not only freebie hunters):

ENTRY RULES (keep it simple)
Option A (best for growth):

- follow
- comment with answer to question
- share to story
- tag 1 friend who would genuinely want this

Option B (best for UGC):

- post a photo using my product
- tag my page
- write 1 sentence about their experience

DURATION
Start date:
End date:
Winner announcement date:

CONTENT PLAN (during giveaway)

- Day 1: announce giveaway + rules
- Day 3: share entries and stories
- Day 5: remind people + show proof of product/service
- Day 7: announce winner + invite inquiries

AFTER GIVEAWAY (the important part)

- Thank everyone
- Feature the best UGC entries (with permission)
- Offer a small "thank you" discount or bonus for serious buyers (optional)
- Send follow-up message to warm leads

MEASUREMENT

- new followers:
- inquiries:
- orders:

- UGC collected:

Appendix K: Weekly Scorecard Template and Review Questions (Copy-ready)

WEEK OF:
MAIN PLATFORM:

SCORECARD
Traffic:

- reach:
- profile visits:
- website visits (if any):

Engagement:

- saves:
- shares:
- comments:
- DMs started:

Inquiries:

- WhatsApp inquiries:
- DMs asking about price/order:
- calls/walk-ins (if relevant):

Conversions:

- orders:
- conversion rate (orders ÷ inquiries):
- revenue:
- average order value:

Repeat/Retention:

- repeat customers:
- repeat rate:

- referrals:
- reviews collected:

Service Quality (optional but powerful):

- on-time delivery rate:
- complaints:
- returns/refunds:

ACTIONS I DID THIS WEEK

- posts published:
- stories posted:
- reels/videos:
- follow-ups sent:
- broadcast sent (yes/no):
- collaborations/partner touches:

WEEKLY REVIEW QUESTIONS

1. What improved this week?
2. What dropped this week?
3. What action likely caused the improvement?
4. What action likely caused the drop?
5. What did customers ask or complain about most?
6. What is one thing I will stop doing?
7. What is one change I will test next week?
8. What is the one priority for next week?

WEEKLY EXPERIMENT
Hypothesis:
One change I will test:
How I will measure:
Decision next week: keep / adjust / drop

BACK MATTER
Final Note to the Reader

If you reached this far, I want to speak to you like a real person, not like a brand.

You did not just read a book about marketing. You stepped into a way of thinking and working that can change your relationship with business. And that matters because business is not only money. Business is time, identity, discipline, and the ability to stand on your own feet in a world that keeps shifting.

I know what it feels like to build with limited resources, unstable internet, and heavy responsibilities. I know what it feels like to want progress but also want peace. I know what it feels like to be full of ideas yet struggle to create a system that holds those ideas in place. That is why I wrote this the way I did: practical, direct, and built around routines you can actually sustain.

Here is the truth I want you to carry forward.

You do not need a perfect plan.
You need a repeatable process.

You do not need to master every platform.
You need to master consistency on one platform and build a base that can support expansion later.

You do not need to copy influencers.
You need to clarify your offer, serve your customers well, and become known for reliability.

People do not buy because you are loud. They buy because you are clear and trustworthy.

If your business is small right now, do not despise that stage. Small is where you learn. Small is where you prove your standard. Small is where you build reputation. But do not remain stuck in "small" forever. Use the sprints. Track your results. Run experiments.

Improve one thing per week. And as you grow, do not lose your peace.

Peace is not laziness. Peace is focus.

The internet rewards speed, but life rewards stability. The businesses that last are the ones built on discipline, clarity, and customer trust. That is why you saw me repeat the same ideas in different forms: offer clarity, audience focus, proof, systems, follow-up, tracking, and testing. Those are not trendy words. Those are survival skills.

If you take one thing from this book, let it be this:

Build a business you can run even on your worst week.

Because life will test you. Your internet will fail sometimes. Your energy will drop sometimes. Customers will complain sometimes. Competitors will appear. Platforms will change. But if your business is built on systems, you will not collapse every time the world moves.

Start small. Stay consistent. Measure what matters. Improve with evidence. Serve people well. That is how you grow without becoming desperate.

Thank you for letting me guide you.

Now go and do the work. One sprint at a time.

Leave a Review

If this book helped you, I have one small request.

Please leave a short review.

Even one or two sentences is enough. Tell other readers what you learned and who you think this book is for. Reviews help more people find the book, and they help me keep writing practical guides like this.

Thank you.

Order and Bulk Copies (training and teams)

If you are a:

Business trainer
School or college program coordinator
Entrepreneurship coach
Community organization
Church or youth group leader
Company training manager
Team leader building a sales or marketing team

You can order bulk copies of this book for training, workshops, and team learning.

Bulk orders work well for:
Entrepreneurship classes
Digital marketing bootcamps
Staff training and onboarding
Youth empowerment programs
Women's groups and savings groups
Community business training
Small business owner workshops

If you want to use this book as a training tool, here are three recommended ways:

Option 1: The 7-day setup sprint workshop
Use the first sprint to help participants build offers, profiles, and first posts.

Option 2: The 30-day consistency sprint challenge
Use the second sprint as a group accountability challenge.

Option 3: The 90-day growth sprint program
Use the final sprint as a complete business building program with weekly reviews and experiments.

For bulk and training orders, contact the author through the contact details provided on the author page and official platforms.

About the Author

John Monyjok Maluth, also known as Panyim, is an entrepreneur, writer, and digital business teacher focused on practical empowerment. He writes for people building from real-life constraints, not perfect conditions. His work emphasizes clarity, discipline, and systems that help ordinary people create stable income and personal freedom through online business.

He has lived and worked across multiple countries and communities, and his writing is shaped by firsthand experience with uncertainty, migration, and rebuilding. That lived reality informs his teaching style: direct, simple, and grounded in what works.

John's mission is to help people move from survival to meaning by building skills, creating assets, and serving customers with integrity. His broader work includes guides on entrepreneurship, digital literacy, writing, self-publishing, and personal discipline.

www.ingramcontent.com/pod-product-compliance
Lightning Source LLC
Chambersburg PA
CBHW031618210526
45464CB00004B/1633